The Price Guide
to the
Models of W.H. Goss

by Roland Ward

The Price Guide
to the
Models of W. H. Goss

by Roland Ward

ANTIQUE COLLECTORS' CLUB

ISBN   0 902028 20 0

Published for the Antique Collectors' Club by the
Antique Collectors' Club Ltd.

Printed in England by
Baron Publishing, Woodbridge, Suffolk.

To my wife Jessie, who showed so much patience and tolerance, during the many evenings and weekends I spent on the preparation of this book.

Why not join the
Antique Collectors' Club

The Antique Collectors' Club was formed in 1966 and now has a five figure membership spread throughout the world. It publishes the only independently run monthly antiques magazine *Antique Collecting* which caters for those collectors who are interested in widening their knowledge of antiques, both by increasing the members' knowledge of quality as well as in discussing the factors which influence the price that is likely to be asked. The Antique Collectors' Club pioneered the provision of information on prices for collectors and the magazine still leads in the provision of detailed articles on a variety of subjects.

It was in response to the enormous demand for information on "what to pay" that the price guide series was introduced in 1968 with the first edition of *The Price Guide to Antique Furniture* (completely revised, 1978), a book which broke new ground by illustrating the more common types of antique furniture, the sort that collectors could buy in shops and at auctions, rather than the rare museum pieces which had previously been used (and still to a large extent are used) to make up the limited amount of illustrations in books published by commercial publishers. Many other price guides have followed, all copiously illustrated, and greatly appreciated by collectors for the valuable information they contain, quite apart from prices. The Antique Collectors' Club also publishes other books on antiques, including horology and art reference works, and a full book list is available.

Club membership, which is open to all collectors, costs £8.95 per annum. Members receive free of charge *Antique Collecting,* the Club's magazine (published every month except August), which contains well-illustrated articles dealing with the practical aspects of collecting not normally dealt with by magazines. Prices, features of value, investment potential, fakes and forgeries are all given prominence in the magazine.

Among other facilities available to members are private buying and selling facilities, the longest list of "For Sales" of any antiques magazine, an annual ceramics conference and the opportunity to meet other collectors at their local antique collectors' clubs. There are nearly eighty in Britain and so far a dozen overseas. Members may also buy the Club's publications at special pre-publication prices.

As its motto implies, the Club is an amateur organisation designed to help collectors to get the most out of their hobby: it is informal and friendly and gives enormous enjoyment to all concerned.

For Collectors — By Collectors — About Collecting
Antique Collectors' Club, 5 Church Street, Woodbridge, Suffolk

Price Revision List

1st November annually

The usefulness of a book containing prices rapidly diminishes as market values change.

In order to keep the prices in this book fully up-dated a revised price list will be issued on 1st November each year. This list will contain the current values of all the pieces illustrated in the book.

To ensure that you receive the Price Revision List yearly, complete a banker's order form and send it to the Antique Collectors' Club now.

The Price Revision List costs £1.25 a year by banker's order or £1.50 cash, from:—

**THE ANTIQUE COLLECTORS' CLUB
WOODBRIDGE, SUFFOLK.**

Colour Plate 2.

Top Row:
Pompeian Ewer, No. 229. **Worcester Jug,** No. 302. **Whitby Ammonite,** No. 291.

Centre:
Cat and Fiddle Inn, No. 425.

Bottom Row:
Mons Meg, No. 204. **Winchester Jack,** No. 295. **Coronation Chair,** No. 76.

Acknowledgements

It would be ingratitude not to show appreciation to the many collectors who have so kindly and freely given their time and supplied information. To those who have allowed items from their collections to be photographed, without which this book would not have been possible in its present form, I am deeply indebted.

It would be impracticable to mention everyone, but it should be recorded that of those members of the Goss Collectors' Club who were willing and able to assist, the following should be specifically mentioned: John Galpin, Michael Norman, Edward Stansmore, John Woodhead, Maurice Regnard, George Reid, George Vaughan and the secretary, Margaret Latham. My special thanks to these and to everyone who has helped in however small a way.

Despite the great amount of assistance given it will be seen that a little information is still lacking. I should be pleased to hear from any reader who can assist with these deficiencies.

Contents

Introduction

Since the last war there has been a great deal of interest in antiques in general, and more recently in Victoriana and even later material. It is in the latter category that most of the models made by the firm of W.H. Goss belong, and they have not only been shown the same interest as contemporary collectable items, but have been enjoying a popularity which probably exceeds that of all others.

This popularity is more evident in the 'named' models than for non-models, such as table-ware, or pieces for other utilitarian purposes. The description 'named' model is used to describe those that bear, either on base or side, some details about the piece. In this book the text, as shown on each model, is given below the title by which that model is usually known. For instance, you will find the model CHESTERFIELD MUG, showing the printing on the base as 'MODEL OF "BRAMPTON WARE" MUG FOUND ON A BEAM DURING REPAIRS TO ROOF OF CHESTERFIELD CHURCH: THE ORIGINAL BEING LEFT BY WORKMEN IN 1750'. A few models without inscriptions are included, mainly in the 'Animals' Section, as they were so obviously suitable for inclusion in the various groups due to their similarity with models, with inscription, in the same section.

The object of this book is to give collectors, and would-be collectors, a record of the items available and also some indication of the value.

Although W.H. Goss was particularly well known for 'Crested China' pieces, many beautiful models were made in natural colours without a Coat of Arms. And although many of those with 'Crest' are extremely scarce, it is the coloured models that are most eagerly sought after, and command a much higher price in almost every instance, due, of course, to the usually accepted principle of supply and demand.

Collecting Goss china was contemporary with its production, and in the first year or so of this century, the League of Goss Collectors was formed by a J.J. Jarvis of Enfield, Middlesex for a select number of acquaintances. Around 1906 the League was opened up to the general public. Mr. Jarvis was not only personally responsible for its formation but for its subsequent management. At first the firm did not co-operate with him and refused to make known the list of the firm's agents in towns and cities throughout the United Kingdom. After initial difficulties, and possibly because the names and addresses were being obtained by less direct methods, W.H. Goss commenced co-operating fully with the League, and subsequently started giving not only the details of agents but of new models in preparation or production. All relative information was given in the 'Goss Record', which was the official magazine of Mr. Jarvis's organisation. Incidentally, very few copies of the 'Goss Record' have survived and at the present time bring a price of £10 to £12, although as much as £15 has been paid.

In 1918 the name was changed to the International League of Goss Collectors, and readers will find in this book models that were issued exclusively to members of both Leagues, and these bear a composite Coat of Arms of either of them. It is not clear when the latter organisation ceased to exist, but as the last model to be issued to members was dated 1932, and it had been the practice for the last fifteen years to issue them annually, it appears safe to assume that that was the last year.

Therefore, there was no organisation to represent collectors for thirty-eight years, until October 1970, when the Goss Collectors' Club was formed and a monthly or bi-monthly Newsletter sent out regularly to members. The Club is not a commercial group but purely for the mutual benefit of members, and it is fair to claim that it has played a big part in the hobby's current popularity. Anyone interested in obtaining details of membership should write to the Secretary, 3 Carr Hall Gardens, Barrowford, Nelson, Lancs.

Particular attention should be given to the short chapter on 'Factors that Determine Values', because despite its brevity it gives the beginner an insight into the pitfalls to be avoided, and some idea of how much should come off a price if the piece is damaged in any way. Early disappointments are to be avoided, as they often result in a new starter to the hobby losing interest. And one of the aims of this book is to encourage the collecting of these delightful models of particularly high quality.

In a few cases it is difficult to draw the line between model and non-model. Where there is doubt, the piece has been included for the collector himself to decide whether, or not, he should accept the piece as a model or reject it.

In the later years of the firm and after control had passed from the Goss family, a few new models were issued, and these are generally marked 'W.H. Goss England' in two lines under the usual Goshawk mark. These models are much cruder, as a general rule, but are included here for the purpose of making the book complete. The appropriate items will be marked to show that they come in this category. In many cases these models are quite scarce and command a high price.

William Henry Goss
and the Firm that bears his name

When, on the 30th July 1833, Sophia Goss (née Mann), the wife of Richard Goss, gave birth to her third son, few, if any, could have foreseen that the child was to give immortality, if not to himself; then certainly to his surname.

William Henry Goss, as the boy was named, grew to be a diligent and intelligent student. It is thought that he received his early training in art at the Government School of Design, which had recently been established in Somerset House. As a result of his studies and the merit he was achieving in art, he was introduced to the then Lord Mayor of London, Alderman William Copeland, who owned the large pottery firm at Stoke-on-Trent that previously belonged to Josiah Spode.

Under the guidance of Copeland, Goss quickly learnt the art of potting and became acquainted with the new medium of Parian ware, which was to be the material the Goss firm worked in for almost the whole of its commercial life. Parian was used to resemble marble toned by age, and was mainly used for busts and figures. He also worked in terra cotta, becoming the chief designer for the Copeland firm, although very little is known of the actual work he did for them and he left to commence business on his own in 1858, at the early age of twenty-five.

At the beginning he partnered a Mr. Peake, at Eastwood Vale, Hanley, although the site of the factory is unknown. This partnership is recorded in Llewellyn Jewitt's "The Ceramic Art of Great Britain", but little is known, and the only specimen of their work is a terra cotta tobacco-jar. Rightly, or wrongly, it is generally assumed that they worked with this medium only. This partnership was extremely short-lived, and after only a few months W.H. Goss commenced working on his own. The mark for the partnership was GOSS & PEAKE, in black.

Working on his own account, he started at a factory believed to have been in John Street, Stoke-on-Trent, although this view is not shared by all authorities. What is certain is that twelve years later, in 1870, he had his own factory off London Road. This was to become the famous Falcon Works, and to see the inception of the Goss family crest as the trade mark. Although a Patent Office Register records an entry dated 26th April 1909 stating that the mark had been in use 'continuously since thirteen years before the August 13th 1875', it does not appear to have been used on the firm's products until the 1880s. Maybe it was used in the early years on their stationery only. When it was first used is therefore in doubt, but what is known is that it was used on models from when they were first made in the early 1890s until the business ceased trading at the start of the Second World War.

Many early pieces attributed to W.H. Goss were unmarked and generally were similar to the products of the Copeland factory. It is considered possible that they were intentionally left unmarked so as to pass as products of the latter maker. Most ardent Goss collectors will find this hard to accept, but we must face the fact that it was some years before Goss established himself and that he had to sell his wares in the meantime. As the Copeland factory was enjoying great popularity, it seems feasible that wares made almost identical to theirs would sell better, without a name, than those carrying a name unknown to the public, a name that was to mean nothing of consequence in ceramics for years to come. It is a fact that, even if the former assumption is incorrect, none of Goss's products after the first fifteen years or so were intentionally sold unmarked. As a guide, collectors should only pay

Goss prices for pieces with one of the Goss marks and a very much lower price for unmarked pieces; although it can often be assumed that a piece could be Goss, it would be unwise to pay other than the price it would command as non-Goss.

Adolphus William Henry Goss, son of W.H., joined in the management of the firm in the early 1880s, and it was through his influence that cheaper lines were introduced, although they continued to make the more expensive lines for which they had become famous. Within the next ten years, and in keeping with the practice of making cheaper lines, the models which are the subject of this book were being made. These were either white-glazed, with a Coat of Arms, or other decoration; or white un-glazed without decoration; or coloured, as in the case of cottages, etc..

By 1883 the father was playing a lesser role and, although the credit for starting to make 'crested' china may well belong to him, there is little doubt that the son was mainly responsible for the change in policy that made these wares the product for which the firm was, and is, best known.

In 1893 the first 'cottage' in coloured Parian ware was made and the first three were Anne Hathaway's, Robert Burns's, and Shakespeare's, to be followed by some thirty-seven more over a period of nearly fifty years. If a model was popular, as were the three cottages mentioned, it was made continuously until the firm ceased trading. This, naturally, necessitated the use of many moulds and many mixings of colours, which leads to a host of variations that are too numerous to attempt to list. Only the major changes will be recorded. The variations in the moulds also account for differences in the white 'crested' pieces, and it is not unusual for pieces to vary in height up to a quarter of an inch. The sizes given are therefore approximate.

William Henry Goss died on the 4th January 1906 and, although in his later years he had taken a much smaller part in the firm's administration, his death was a blow to the firm. Adolphus Goss insisted that his legacy be paid at once and this left the firm short of ready cash, which naturally was an embarrassment for some considerable time. He left everything connected with the business to his two youngest sons, Victor Henry and William Huntley Goss, Adolphus William Henry Goss, who had pioneered the more reasonably priced products, apparently retiring from the business. It was the death, through a riding accident, in March 1913, of Captain Victor H. Goss, that proved to be a set-back from which the Goss family and business never really recovered.

Business kept prospering up to the start of the First World War, when, naturally, there was a recession, although both the popular old models and new ones were made during the period of hostilities. After the war and due to the ever-changing trends, their products began to lose popularity, until in 1928 the position was so bad that they were facing bankruptcy, and negotiations were begun with interested parties for the sale of stock, goodwill, premises and equipment, in a last desperate attempt to avoid that calamity. This, eventually, resulted in the firm being sold in 1929 to George Jones & Sons Ltd., who had previously acquired several other china firms who made 'crested' china, such as Swan, Arcadian, Crescent, etc. Some authorities are of the opinion that the quality of the models deteriorated from the date of transfer of power. This is not so, and evidence is in existence to point to business being conducted as usual at least up to the end of 1931. For instance, pieces were made for the International League of Goss Collectors, in the same quality, right up to the one dated 1932, which, presumably, was made late in 1931. It would seem, therefore, that it was after the latter date, when in fact the firm became Wm. H. Goss Ltd., that radical changes took place and the mark 'England' was added under W.H. Goss on the mark.

Because of the circumstances mentioned at the end of the last paragraph, it has been decided not to exclude completely from this 'Price Guide' those pieces that carry the new mark, although they are mainly listed in the appendix. The usual reason given by those who reject these from their collections is that they were made after control of the firm had left the Goss family, but few seem to reject the three International League pieces for the same reason.

From 1935 the firm was known as the Goss China Co. Ltd., although it was still being made at the famous Falcon Works. Shortly after this the empire of George Jones and Sons Ltd. collapsed and the Goss assets were acquired by Cauldron Potteries Ltd. around 1936-7. In the later years from sometime between 1931 and 1935, up to production ceasing in 1940, the quality of the models was poor, and it was during this period that the word ENGLAND is usually found below the mark, although many examples of late ware were not marked in that way. Many of the items made during this period were completely new and others were old models made from entirely new moulds, whilst others were identical with models bearing the maker's name of other companies in the group.

Cauldron Potteries were eventually absorbed into the Coalport Group, who retained the right to use the Goss trade mark and all other assets of the company. In July 1954, Messrs. Ridgeway Potteries Ltd. acquired all the assets including moulds, patterns, designs etc., as well as the right to use the Goss name and trade mark. At the moment this is the end of the story and it remains to be seen if the present owners ever commence to make 'Goss' wares again.

In this book of models it is not thought correct to list all the markings used by the firm, and it is sufficient to say that models from 1883-1931 carried the mark of the Goshawk with the name W.H. GOSS beneath, and that most of those models produced later additionally carried the word ENGLAND beneath the name. Many early models additionally carry an impressed mark W.H. GOSS as well as the printed mark. The new models made after 1922 additionally carry the word COPYRIGHT. A common fallacy that pieces without the word ENGLAND were made before 1891 certainly does not apply to Goss, although ceramic authorities have given this impression in many books over the last half century, John Galpin, in his excellent book 'Goss China', being the first, to the author's knowledge, to refute this completely. Models first made between 1905 and 1914 usually also carry the Registration Number, although a few, particularly cottages, carry them from as early as 1884, the first being 208047, Anne Hathaway's Cottage. They continued to carry the number right through to the end of the firm.

Points Affecting Prices

1.

The following increase price: –

(a) **Correct Crests**   These usually command a price increase between 25%-50%, and an example would be Aberdeen Coats of Arms on model no. 1, Aberdeen Bronze Pot. Care must be taken with the few models that can only be found with an appropriate crest.

(b) **Military and Naval Badges.** Keenly sought after and scarce. £10-£30 should be added, depending upon rarity.

(c) **Transfer Prints**   Many models carry one colour transfer prints and they make a very attractive addition to any collection. They can be found in the following colours, which vary in their range:—

Black, Brown (Sepia), Red, Blue and Green

This decoration adds from £15-£30 depending on size and colour. The first three colours mentioned are the most common; green and blue are both extremely scarce.

(d) **Trusty Servant**   This attractive decoration is found on many pieces, but is one of the appropriate emblems for Winchester models, on the larger of which it also carries the inscription from the wall of Winchester. This emblem would add £15 to the value of a piece.

(e) **Commemoratives**   Naturally these are collected not only by Goss addicts but also by those who collect Commemorative china irrespective of maker. This affects the price and would make Goss Commemorative pieces worth quadruple for better known events, such as Queen Victoria's Jubilee and George V's Coronation, and even more for events when smaller numbers were made such as those for the Preston Guild, which were probably only sold through the Preston agent.

(f) **Miscellaneous Decorations**   Many other decorations can be found and they all add to the value of the piece to varying degrees. Because of the variety and the large number of models they are found on, it is not easy to give an exact value but collectors would be safe in adding £10-£30 to the price they would pay for models with Coats of Arms.

Some of the decorations found are:—

Forget-me-nots
Thistles
Butterflies
'A Present From . . .'
Shamrocks
Welsh Antiquities
Animals
Birds, etc., etc..

2.   **Factors that would reduce the value of pieces**

The prices given in this book are for perfect pieces only, and the slightest sign of damage or wear detracts considerably from the value. The following would detract from value:—

(a) **Cracks and Chips** A crack or break in a common piece, however slight the damage, would make anything, priced at £5 or less, worthless. Rarer models would come down to about half for damage that could be well repaired, to around a quarter for more extensive damage.

(b) **Repairs** There has been some controversy over the value of repaired items, one school choosing to consider them practically worthless, whilst others still put a high value on them, even up to 90% of the price of a perfect piece. Many points are certain but to give but two — first, there are many collectors who have repaired models in their collections and are unaware of the fact that they have been restored to their previous perfect state, at least in appearance. Secondly, collectors are prepared to buy these rarer models in repaired condition and pay high prices for them. If you need a lamp to determine the state of a piece that looks perfect, then it is extremely unlikely that you would buy anything, as one could hardly take it round antique shops and auctions.

(c) **Gold Rims** Any wear at all on the rim does spoil the appearance of a piece and serious collectors would disregard them completely. If you must buy them, half price is probably reasonable.

(d) **Worn and Discoloured Decorations** As far as price is concerned, these fall in the same category as worn gilt on the rim. These come about by wear, fading or oxidization of the colours.

(f) **Lids.** Where a model should have a lid, collectors are strongly advised to purchase even if it is missing. Many are looking, and even advertising for, lids to complete models but they are rarely found.

Forged Marks

and

Forgeries

Recently pieces have been found with forged 'Goshawk' marks, and the new or unsuspecting collector could easily fall victim to this illegal practice. It is difficult to lay down rules to help detect all these false marks.

To the experienced and well-established collector the problem is not serious and it is to others that these notes are particularly directed.

As this book is solely concerned with models, we must keep to these as far as forged marks go. The first rule therefore is to reject 'models' that do not bear descriptions of the piece, remembering that almost all the domestic ware and many decorative items do not carry descriptions at all. Secondly, all specific models, such as a gramophone or bulldog, both recorded with forged marks, must be rejected if they are not included in this book. Further, most of the pieces used for putting the spurious mark on were anonymous and consequently of a standard much below the wares of W.H. Goss. Reject all very crude models.

In an effort to detect the forgeries, it should be noted that these marks are often also very crude and, for some reason, distorted. Close inspection mostly shows that the ground below the mark appears to be of a very slightly different texture, not noticeable in genuine ones.

Over the years, we have grown accustomed to new models being discovered and it is extremely unlikely that we have now recorded them all. It is difficult to say that unrecorded specimens have forged marks but it is prudent to doubt these newcomers. Most of these that have been done to defraud collectors have been on models that would not deceive a serious collector, as the models used have been in the main crude anonymous models that the maker did not deem warranted his name. We know that some 'crested' china is quite good, to mention only Willow Art and Arcadian. These do not appear to have been used. Maybe removing the existing mark was considered an unnecessary exercise.

One point to remember is that the 'GOSS/ENGLAND' mark has not as yet been recorded forged.

MISCELLANEOUS

No. 1. Aberdeen Bronze Pot

Inscribed: Model of bronze pot found in Upperkirkgate Aberdeen May 31st, 1886. Containing 12267 pennies.

It can be found without reference to the pennies, the inscription finishing at 1886.

(a)	height	64mm.	Price	£4
(b)	height	83mm.	Price	£6.50
(c)	height	185mm.	Price	£20

The original, which is Roman, was decorated with fine moulding that is far from clear on the model.

No. 2. Abergavenny Jar

Inscribed: Model of ancient jar found at Abergavenny. Rd. No. 633432.

height 54mm. Price £3.75

The original, found on the then site of Lloyd's Bank, Abergavenny, is of great antiquity, and believed to date back to before the Roman Empire.

No. 3. Abingdon Roman Vase

Inscribed: Model of roman vase dug up at The Abbey, Abingdon.

height 95mm. Price £15

The correct Coat of Arms on this model makes the piece particularly attractive and would in this case add 50% to the value.

No. 4. Alnwick Sepulchral Urn

Inscribed: Model of Celtic urn dug up at Alnwick.

height 68mm. Price £6.50

The original, dug up in the town in 1824, is believed to be of great antiquity and almost 2,000 years old. It has a beautiful outline and the incised decoration is effective.

No. 5. Amersham Leaden Measure

Inscribed: Model of leaden measure circa 1682, found in the old lock up in the Town Hall, Amersham. Rd. No. 626749.

height   48mm.   Price   £7.50

No. 6. Antwerp Oolen Pot

Inscribed: Model of Oolen pot 16th century. Found inside a Caisson at Antwerp. Now in Liebaert Museum at Ostend. Rd. No. 495668.

Correct Coats of Arms: Antwerp and two other Belgian arms in the two other panels.

height   70mm.   Price   £4

No. 7. Appleby Bushel

Inscribed: Model of Elizabethan bushel measure now in Appleby Moot Hall.

diameter   59mm.   Price   £11.50

The original is of solid bronze with a diameter of 1ft. 7¼ins. and weighing 69½lbs.

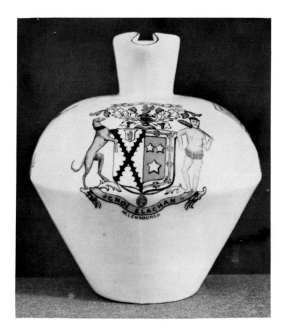

No. 8. Arundel Ewer

Inscribed: Model of Roman ewer, found at Avisford Hill, Arundel.

(a)   height   55mm.   Price   £6
(b)   height   105mm.   Price   £10

Although not obvious from the photograph, this model has a small handle.

No. 9. Ashbourne Bushel

Inscribed: Model of Ashbourne bushel. Rd. No. 450628.

diameter   51mm.   Price   £6

No. 10. Ashley Rails Urn

Inscribed: Model of Roman urn found at Ashley Rails, New Forest. Copyright.

height   108mm.   Price   £25

It is not clear which Coats of Arms would be most appropriate to this model.

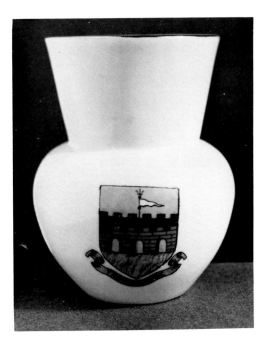

No. 11. Avebury Celtic Urn

Inscribed: Model of Celtic urn, dug up near Avebury.

height   105mm.   Price   £11.50

The original was found in a Celtic grave near the great stone circle at Avebury.

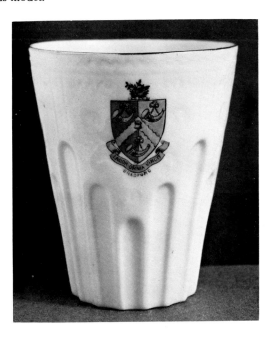

No. 12. Ballafletcher Cup

Inscribed: Model of the Lhannan Shee (peaceful spirit) Cup of Ballafletcher, in the possession of J.C. Bacon, Esq., Seafield, Isle of Man. Rd. No. 448432.

height   95mm.   Price   £20

The original, of glass, was looted from St. Olaf's Shrine in Trondhjem and the name Ballafletcher was given to it when it came into the possession of the Fletcher family in 1580. An interesting passage is included in C.W. Airne's "The Story of the Isle of Man", volume 2.

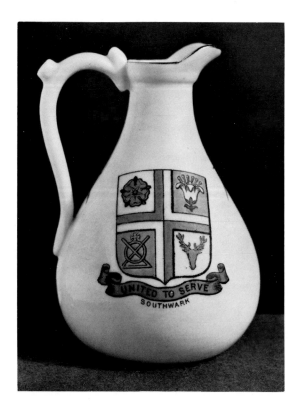

No. 13. Bartlow Ewer

Inscribed: Model of Roman bronze ewer found in 1835 at Bartlow Hills, near Saffron Walden.

Correct Coats of Arms: Saffron Walden.

        height   104mm.   Price   £15

Found with many other Roman objects in 1835 in an artificial mound at Bartlow Hills.

No. 14. Bath Bronze Ewer

Inscribed: From bronze original found in Roman bath at Bath.

      height   120mm.   Price   £15.50

No. 15. Bath Roman Cup

Inscribed: Model of ancient Roman cup found at Bath. Rd. No. 543009.

      height to top of handles   102mm.   Price   £85

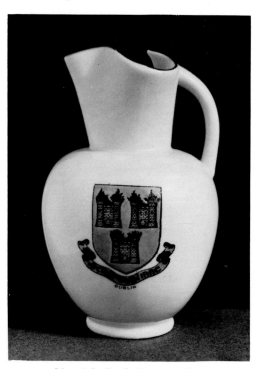

No. 16. Bath Roman Ewer

Inscribed: Model of bath Roman ewer in Dorset Museum. Found at Bath.

(a)   height   65mm.   Price   £3.50
(b)   height   123mm.   Price   £10

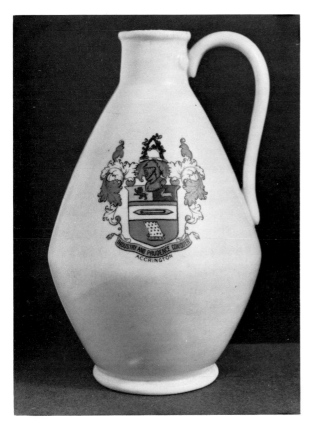

No. 17. Bath Roman Jug

Inscribed: Model of Roman jug, found at the Roman bath at Bath.

height   150mm.   Price   £19.50

No. 18. Bath Urn

Inscribed: The bath urn from original in Museum.

height   75mm.   Price   £10

No. 19. Bettws-y-coed Kettle

Inscribed: Model of ancient bronze kettle dug up near Bettws-y-coed 1877. Rd. No. 543011.

(a)   height   72mm.   Price   £6.50
(b)   height   110mm.   Price   £12.50

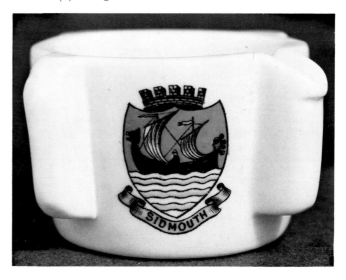

No. 20. Bideford Mortar

Inscribed: Model of ancient mortar dredged out of the Torridge at Bideford. Rd. No. 622407.

height   42mm.   Price   £8.50

The original, which was at the Goss works at the time the model was made and probably became part of the collection of W.H. Goss, was found by fishermen after repairs to the bridge.

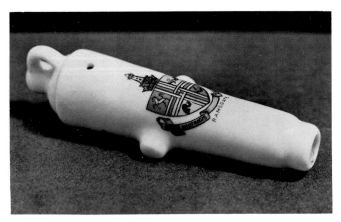

No. 21. Blackgang Cannon

Inscribed: Model of ancient cannon found on the beach at Blackgang Chine, I.W. Rd. No. 554472.

length   95mm.   Price   £6.50

No. 22. Bolton Abbey Wine Cooler

Inscribed: Model of wine cooler at Bolton Abbey. Rd. No. 633428.

diameter 68mm.   Price   £14.50

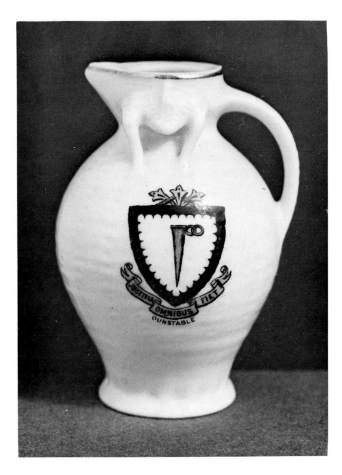

No. 23. Boston Ewer

Inscribed: Model of ancient ewer now in Boston Museum. Rd. No. 594871.

height   70mm.   Price   £6

The original, intact with the exception of the handle, was in the Municipal Buildings in 1921. It is an old Saxon jar which was found when excavating for Boston Dock, Lincolnshire.

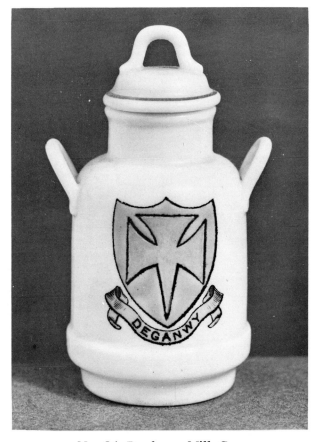

No. 24. Boulogne Milk Can

Inscribed: Model of Boulogne milk can. Rd. No. 521974.

height   74mm.   Price   £10

It should not be bought without lid as in that state it would be practically worthless.

No. 25. Boulogne Sedan Chair

Inscribed: Model of sedan chair used by the Countess of Boulogne. Rd. No. 539423.

height   69mm.   Price   £30

A contemporary advertisement offers this piece decorated in turquoise blue, but a coloured one has not yet been recorded.

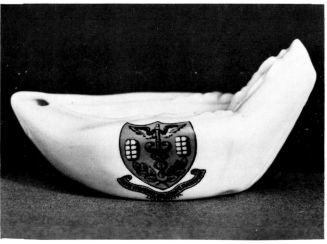

No. 26. Bournemouth Egyptian Lamp

Inscribed: Model of ancient Egyptian lamp circa B.C. 100 to A.D. 100. Found at Southbourne, Bournemouth. Rd. No. 638371.

length   105mm.   Price   £12

No. 27. Bournemouth Mace Head

Inscribed: Model of ancient bronze mace head circa A.D. 300. Found in King's Park, Bournemouth. Rd. No. 613962.

height   80mm.   Price   £12

No. 28. Bournemouth Pilgrim Bottle

Inscribed: Model of Pilgrim bottle (circa 600 A.D.). Found at Southbourne, Bournemouth 1907. Rd. No. 562740.

height   90mm.   Price   £6.50

As the original was only found in 1907 it is easier to date this model than most as it was recorded for the first time in the "Goss Record" of 1913-14.

No. 29. Bournemouth Urn

Inscribed: Model of ancient bronze urn in the Museum of the Royal Bath Hotel, Bournemouth.

height   52mm.   Price   £6.50

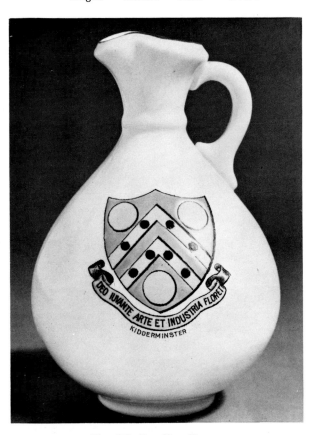

No. 30. Brading Ewer

Inscription: Model of ewer found on site of Roman villa, Brading, I.O.W.

(a)   height   66mm.   Price   £6
(b)   height   118mm.   Price   £8.50

Found on the site of the Roman villa at Morton, near Brading. The villa, dating from around 250-260 a.d. was discovered in April 1880.

No. 31. Brading Stocks

Inscribed: Model of the stocks, Brading, I.O.W. Copyright.

length   87mm.   Price   £225

All known models have the stocks coloured brown (natural colour?) and the base white.

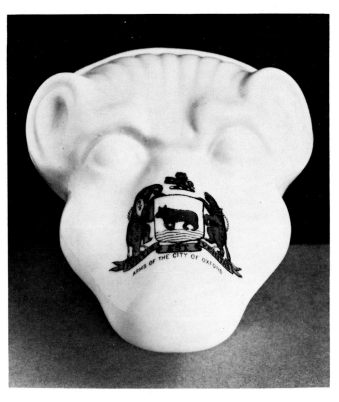

No. 32. Brazenose

Inscribed: The nose of Brazenose, Oxford.

height   104mm.   Price   £16

Modelled from the ancient knocker at Brazenose College, Oxford. It can be found without Coats of Arms, and is rare thus.

No. 33. Bridlington Quart Measure

Inscribed: Model of Bridlington quart measure now in "The Old Bayle Gate", Bridlington. Rd. No. 509868.

height 50mm. Price £5.50

A pleasing little model, which is embossed "E.R. 1601" on the side not shown in the photograph.

No. 34. Bristol Puzzle Cider Cup

Inscribed: Model of puzzle cider cup made at the Bristol Pottery 1791. Now in Bristol Museum. Rd. No. 562739.

Correct Coats of Arms: City of Bristol
      See of Bristol   All on the
      Clifton College   same model
      Bristol University

height 51mm. Price £12.50

It is possible that this model can be found with less than four Coats of Arms but the normal piece shows one in each quarter.

No. 35. Brixworth Cup

Inscribed: Model of ancient cup found at Brixworth, Northamptonshire. Rd. No. 423199.

Correct Coats of Arms: Northampton.

height 55mm. Price £4

The Brixworth Cup is the oldest piece of sun-dried pottery found in Northamptonshire. In 1913 the original was in Northampton Museum.

No. 36. Burton Beer Barrel

Inscribed: Model of Burton beer barrel.

(a) height 60mm. Price £5.50
(b) height 70mm. Price £6.50

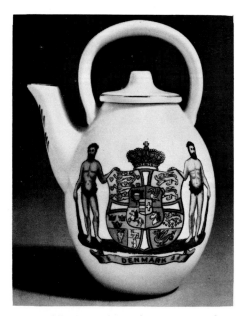

No. 37. Bury St. Edmunds Kettle

Inscribed: Model of Roman libation vessel found at Suffolk. Now in Bury Museum.

(a)	height	75mm.	Price	£10
(b)	height	122mm.	Price	£18.50

At the time the model was made the original was in Bury St. Edmunds Museum and bore the label "Roman vessel used for libation at sacrifices". If it is Roman it was more probably used for oil to fill the small terra cotta lamps, which are found in good numbers on sites of Roman settlements. It is however considered to be Spanish and of a much later date, say the 16th century.

No. 38. Caerhun Urn

Inscribed: Model of Roman burial urn found at Caerhun (Conovium) in 1878 containing calcinated female bones. Copyright.

height 54mm. Price £20

No. 39. Caerleon Lachrymatory

Inscribed: Model of glass lachrymatory or tear bottle found in stone coffin. Discovered in the excavations for the railway, near Caerleon, July 1847. Now in Caerleon Museum. Rd. No. 559520.

height 86mm. Price £4

No. 40. Caerleon Lamp

Inscribed: Model of ancient lamp in Museum at Caerleon (City of Legions, King Arthur's Capital).

length 88mm. Price £4.50

This was one of a large number of Roman Lamps found at Caerleon. From the shape, this one however, may have been made by the Britons after the Romans had left England, and during the period when the arts introduced by the Romans were fast decaying, due to continued civil war.

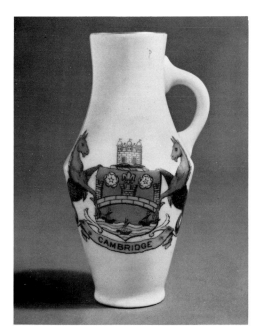

No. 41. Cambridge Pitcher

Inscribed: Model of Cambridge pitcher from original in Archaeological Museum.

    (a)   height   65mm.   Price   £3.50
    (b)   height   115mm.   Price   £6.50

The original, considered to be 14th century, was found near Cambridge in 1864. It was roughly made with traces of green glass on the body.

No. 42. Canary Porren

Inscribed: Model of Canary Porren. Rd. No. 449120.

    height   68mm.   Price   £30

This model is identical to No. 121 Gibraltar Alcaraza.

In the photograph, the Arms are shown on reverse and are invariably Las Palmas, Grand Canary.

No. 43. Canterbury Jug

Inscribed: The Canterbury jug.

    height   113mm.   Price   £8

The original, thought to be of Norman origin, was discovered in 1892 when excavating for the County Hotel, Canterbury.

No. 44. Canterbury Leather Bottle

Inscribed: Model of the Pilgrim 'leather bottell' in Canterbury Museum. Rd. No. 392067.

    height   46mm.   Price   £3.25

Although all record of the original has been lost it was of great age and thought to date back to the Canterbury Pilgrims.

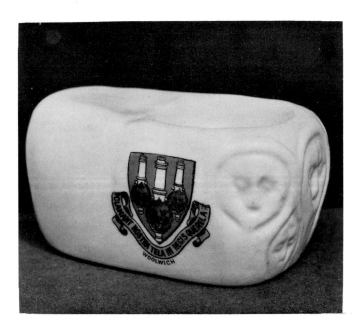

No. 45. Capel Madoc Stoop

Inscribed: Model of stoop from Capel Madoc near Rhayader removed to Dderw, circa 1855. Rd. No. 643962.

length 80mm. Price £18.50

No. 46. Cardinal Beaufort's Candlestick

Inscribed: Model of Cardinal Beaufort's Candlestick. (1404-1447).

height 152mm. Price £110

The originals, of both this model and No. 47 were in bronze and in 1921 were in St. Cross Hospital, Winchester.

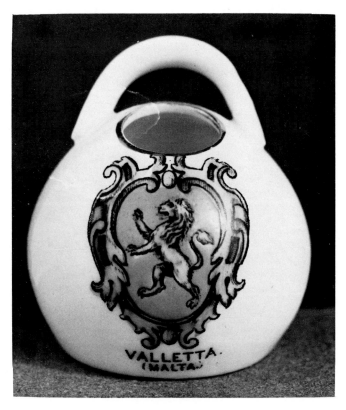

No. 47. Cardinal Beaufort's Salt Cellar

Inscribed: Model of Cardinal Beaufort's salt cellar. (1404-1447).

height 70mm. Price £65

No. 48. Carlisle Salt Pot

Inscribed: Model of old salt pot in Carlisle Museum. Rd. No. 403422.

height 46mm. Price £3

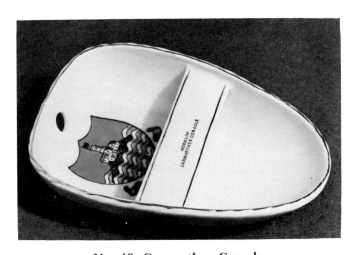

No. 49. Carmarthen Coracle

Inscribed: Model of Carmarthen Coracle.

length 133mm. Price £25

No. 50. Carnarvon Ewer

Inscribed: From original found at Carnarvon. (Roman Segontium), now in Carnarvon Castle.

(a) height 63mm. Price £4.50
(b) height 80mm. Price £6

Segontium was the most important post occupied by the Romans in North Wales and the remains of its walls can be found in gardens outside Caernarvon. In his "Catalogue of British Cities", Nennius calls it Caer Cystenin or the Castle of Constantine.

No. 51. Castletown Urn

Inscribed: Model of cinerary urn found at Gretch Veg I. of Man Jany. 1899. Now in Museum Castle Rushen Castletown I. of Man. Rd. No. 599333.

height 40mm. Price £4

No. 52. Channel Islands Fish Basket

Inscribed: (1) Model of Alderney fish basket. (2) Model of Guernsey fish basket. (3) Model of Jersey fish basket. (4) Model of Sark fish basket.

1	(a)	length	71mm.	Price	£25
	(b)	length	102mm.	Price	£32.50
2	(a)	length	71mm.	Price	£8
	(b)	length	102mm.	Price	£12
3	(a)	length	71mm.	Price	£6.50
	(b)	length	102mm.	Price	£10
*(c)		length	102mm.	Price	£10
4	(a)	length	71mm.	Price	£20
	(b)	length	102mm.	Price	£25

*This model does not bear a Coat of Arms, nor the smooth base that normally carries it. Alderney and Sark models normally have correct Arms.

No. 53. Channel Islands Milk Can

Inscribed: (1) Alderney milk can. (2) Guernsey milk can. (3) Jersey milk can. (4) Sark milk can.

Correct Coats of Arms: Alderney, Guernsey, Jersey and Sark respectively. Alderney and Sark normally carry the correct Arms.

1		height	70mm.	Price	£25
2	(a)	height	70mm.	Price	£8.50
	(b)	height	108mm.	Price	£10
	(c)	height	140mm.	Price	£14.50
3	(a)	height	70mm.	Price	£9.50
	(b)	height	108mm.	Price	£12
	(c)	height	140mm.	Price	£13.50
4		height	70mm.	Price	£20

These models carry moveable lids.

No. 54. Cheddar Cheese

Inscribed: Model of a cheddar cheese. Rd. No. 521975.

(a)	white	height	62mm.	Price	£20
(b)	pale yellow	height	62mm.	Price	£25

This model carries the inscription without the Registered Number on the side as well as on the base.

No. 55. Cherbourg Milk Can

Inscribed: Model of Cherbourg milk can. Rd. No. 605734.

height   65mm.   Price   £15

Of little value unless complete with lid.

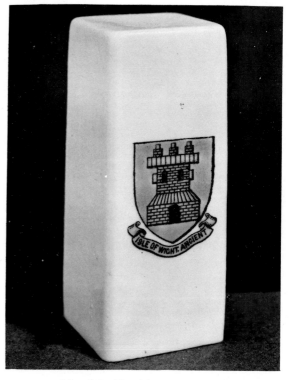

No. 56. Cheshire Salt Block

Inscribed: Model of Cheshire salt block. Copyright.

height   80mm.   Price   £18

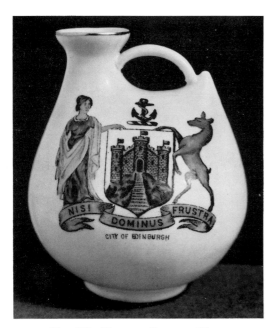

No. 57. Chester Roman Vase

Inscribed: Model of Roman vase found at Chester from the original in museum.

(a)	height	55mm.	Price	£3.25
(b)	height	93mm.	Price	£8

The original was found under the City walls and was kept in King Charles's Tower.

No. 58. Chesterfield Mug

Inscribed: Model of "Brampton Ware" mug found on a beam during repairs to the roof of Chesterfield Church, the original being left by workman in 1750. Copyright.

height   93mm.   Price   £40

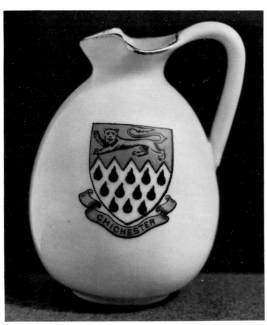

No. 59. Chichester Roman Ewer

Inscribed: Model of Roman Ewer in Chichester Museum. Rd. No. 403420.

height   63mm.   Price   £3.50

The original is in ordinary redware, decorated with six black bands and two circular ornaments in front of, and at either side of, the spout.

No. 60. Chichester Roman Urn

Inscribed: Model of Roman urn found at Chichester now in the museum.

height   81mm.   Price   £6.50

The original, in black Upchurch Ware, was discovered at Chichester when the new Castle Market was set out in 1870-71.

No. 61. Chile Hat

No inscription.

    diameter of rim   86mm.   Price   £250

No. 62. Chile Mate Cup

No inscription.

    height   60mm.   Price   £15

No. 63. Chile Spur

No inscription.

    length   114mm.   Price   £250

No. 64. Chile Stirrup

No inscription.

    height   50mm.   Price   £150

When any of the four Chile pieces carries the Chile Coats of Arms they also show the inscription above. i.e. "Chupaya" meaning hat, "estribo" meaning stirrup, etc. The prices shown are for Coats of Arms other than "Chile". When bearing the latter Arms the price would be 50% more.

No. 65. Christchurch British Bowl

Inscribed: Model of ancient bowl found near Christchurch, Hants. Rd. No. 639533.

diameter 60mm. Price £4

No. 66. Christchurch Urn

Inscribed: Model of Romano-British Urn, found near Christchurch, Hants. Rd. No. 639534.

height 52mm. Price £3.50

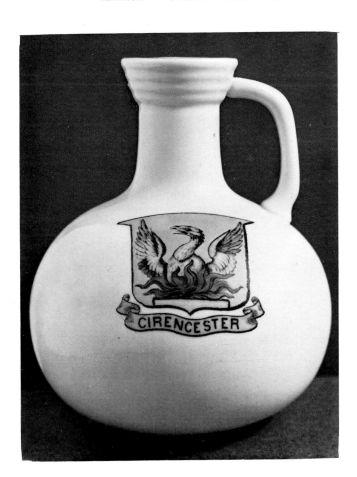

No. 67. Cirencester Roman Ewer

Inscribed: Model of Roman ewer found at Cirencester now in the museum.

height 115mm. Price £30

No. 68. Cirencester Roman Vase

Inscribed: Model of Roman vase found at Cirencester, now in the museum.

(a) height 73mm. Price £4
(b) height 126mm. Price £8.50

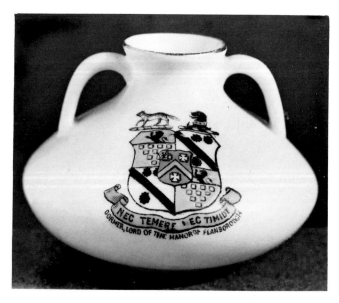

No. 69. Colchester 'Cloaca' Vase

Inscribed: Model of Roman vase found in the 'Cloaca'. Now in Colchester Castle.

diameter   65mm.   Price   £3.50

No. 70. Colchester Gigantic Wine Vase

Inscribed: Model of gigantic Roman wine vase in Colchester Castle. Found in Castle Yard.

height   157mm.   Price   £27.50

The original, standing 4ft. 3ins. high, was reputed to be full of wine when buried.

No. 71. Colchester Vase

Inscribed: The famous Colchester vase in the museum.

(a)   height   42mm.   Price   £3
(b)   height   133mm.   Price   £10

The original was a fine piece of Roman Pottery, ornamented in relief with hunting scenes, figures of gladiators etc.

No. 72. Corfe Castle Cup

Inscribed: Model of ancient cup dug up near Castle Corfe.

height   62mm.   Price   £6.50

This model has a very clumsy handle not visible on the photograph.

No. 73. Cornish Bussa

Inscribed: Model of Cornish bussa. Rd. No. 594377.

height   55mm.   Price   £3.50

The rim on this piece gives the impression that it should carry a lid, but this is not so.

No. 75. Cornish Stile

Inscribed: Model of a Cornish stile. Rd. No. 567378

		length	72mm.	Price	£45
(a)	White	length	72mm.	Price	£45
*(b)	White	length	72mm.	Price	£20
	(Blackpool crest)				
(c)	Brown	length	72mm.	Price	£100

*This type rarely carries the inscription; they are thought to be seconds and that the Blackpool agent was responsible for the Crest.

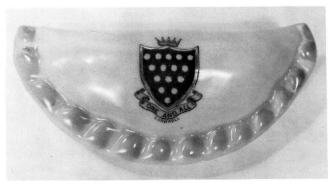

No. 74. Cornish Pasty

Inscribed: Cornish pasty there are so many saints in Cornwall that the devil was afraid to cross the Tamar for fear of being put into a "Cornish Pasty". Ancient Legend.

(a)	Glazed white	length	110mm.	Price	£65
(b)	Glazed yellow	length	110mm.	Price	£100

No. 76. Coronation Chair

Inscribed: Model of the Coronation chair in Westminster Abbey. Rd. No. 578694.

height   87mm.   Price   £22.50

See also Perth Coronation Chair No. 225.

No. 77. Cronk Aust Urn

Inscribed: Model of Cinerary urn from Cronk Aust, Ramsey. Rd. No. 521975.

height   59mm.   Price   £4

The price for this model when produced was 3/-, which is high for small models and dearer than for many of the small coloured buildings.

No. 79. Dartmouth Sack Bottle

Inscribed: Model of sack bottle dredged from the Dart from the original in Exeter Museum.

(a)   height   60mm.   Price   £4
(b)   height   85mm.   Price   £6.50

In 1921 the original was no longer in Exeter Museum but the Catalogue of that date states: "An Old Wine Bottle dredged up in the harbour, Dartmouth, Devon, having on the back of it an embossed Medallion in molten glass with this inscription in relief — Thos. Holdsworth, Dartmouth, 1735". At that time Holdsworth was the Governor of Dartmouth Castle. The inscription can be clearly seen on the better moulded models.

No. 78. Cuckfield Bellarmine

Inscribed: Model of ancient bellarmine found in a pond at Horsgate, Cuckfield. Rd. No. 647236.

height   75mm.   Price   £7

The original, when found, contained spirits. Bellarmines are also known as "Greybeards" due to the fact that the figure of a bearded man is shown on the neck of the vessel. See also Rochester Bellarmine No. 242.

No. 80. Denbigh Brick

Inscribed: Model of a brick found at Denbigh Castle representing the legend of St. Hubert. Date about 1620.

(a)   Glazed white   height   82mm.   Price   £65
(b)   Unglazed white   height   82mm.   Price   £100
(c)   Brown   height   82mm.   Price   £200

The legend is that St. Hubert was out hunting when he met a stag with a cross in its antlers; he dismounted, fell to his knees, and prayed.

No. 81. Devizes Celtic Drinking Cup

Inscribed: Model of Celtic drinking cup found at Devizes.

(a)	height	62mm.	Price	£4
(b)	height	84mm.	Price	£7.50

No. 82. Devon Cider Barrel

Inscribed: Model of Devon Cider barrel. Copyright.

height   60mm.   Price   £8

In design this model is identical to No. 36 Burton Beer Barrel.

No. 83. Devon Cooking Pot

Inscribed: Model of Devon Cooking Pot. Copyright.

height   46mm.   Price   £8

This model is identical to No. 199. Manx Pot.

No. 84. Devon Oak Pitcher

Inscribed: Model of oak pitcher peculiar to Devon.

(a)	height	57mm.	Price	£3.25
(b)	height	108mm.	Price	£11.50

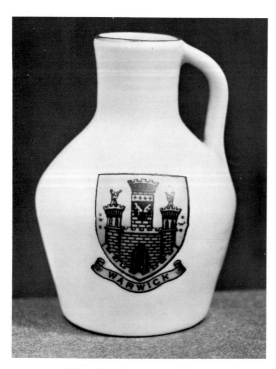

No. 85. Doncaster Ewer

Inscribed: Model of ancient ewer found during excavation at Elephant Hotel, Doncaster, 1914. Copyright.

height 67mm. Price £10

No. 86. Doncaster Urn

Inscribed: Model of ancient urn found in the Market Place Doncaster. Copyright.

height 39mm. Price £6

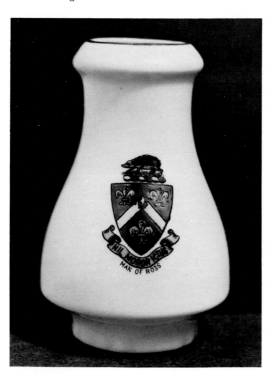

No. 87. Doncaster Vase

Inscribed: Model of ancient vase found in High St., Doncaster. Copyright.

height 78mm. Price £8

No. 88. Dorchester Jug

Inscribed: Model of old jug found in North Sq., Dorchester.

height 50mm. Price £3.25

The original, seven inches high, was found whilst digging a sewer in North Square, Dorchester in 1895. It is Roman Black, miscalled Upchurch Ware.

No. 89. Dorchester Roman Cup

Inscribed: Model of Roman cup (Dorset Museum) found at Dorchester.

(a)	height	48mm.	Price	£3.50
(b)	height	85mm.	Price	£8

A peculiar drinking cup with a groove around the top. The original was thought to have a metal band.

No. 91. Dover Stone Vessel

Inscribed: Model of ancient stone vessel from Dover Castle in Dover Museum.

height   51mm.   Price   £4

This is really a mortar, which, at the time it was made, was in daily use by housewives with any knowledge of herbs. Many of these vessels were carved or ornamented.

No. 90. Dorothy Vernon's Porridge Pot

Inscribed: Model of Dorothy Vernon's porridge pot.

height   72mm.   Price   £7.50

The original, made of wood, was of great age and at the time of the breaking up of the Estate at Haddon Hall it was reputed to have been taken away by a retainer called Dale. In the 1920's it was in the possession of a Mr. John Sleigh.

No. 92. Durham Abbey Knocker

Inscribed: (The) Durham Abbey Knocker.

1	(a)	White flower holder (illus.)	149mm.	Price	£37.50
	(b)	Brown flower holder (illus.)	149mm.	Price	£47.50
2		Night light	83mm.	Price	£100
3	(a)	Two-handled cup	52mm.	Price	£40
	(b)	Two-handled cup	80mm.	Price	£55
	(c)	Two-handled cup	118mm.	Price	£85

None of these models bear Coats of Arms. They are replicas of the original knocker embossed (outpressed) on household items. Each model has different Reg. No.

No. 93. Egyptian Mocha Cup. (Bowl)

Inscribed: Model of Egyptian mocha cup. Rd. No. 572083.

Often found without inscription.

diameter   55mm.   Price   £3

This model bears the same inscription and Registered Number as No. 94.

It may well be that either number 93 or 94 is in fact an error.

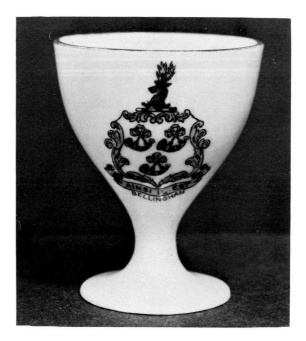

No. 94. Egyptian Mocha Cup. (Egg-cup)

Inscribed: Model of Egyptian Mocha cup. Rd. No. 572083.

Often found without inscription.

height   52mm.   Price   £3

This model bears the same inscription and Registered Number as No. 93.

It may well be that either number 93 or 94 is in fact an error.

No. 95. Egyptian Water Jar

Inscribed: Model of Egyptian water jar. Rd. No. 569836.

height   56mm.   Price   £3.50

No. 96. Egyptian Canopic Jar. No. 1

Inscribed: Model of ancient Egyptian canopic jar with anubis head. No. 1 Copyright.

height with lid   76mm.   Price   £55

This model would be of little or no value without head (lid).

No. 97. Egyptian Kohl Pot. No. 4

Inscribed: Model of Egyptian kohl pot. No. 4 Copyright.

height 66mm. Price £15

No Egyptian models have been found bearing the numbers 2 or 3.

No. 98. Egyptian Kohl Pot. No. 5

Inscribed: Model of ancient Egyptian kohl pot. No. 5 Copyright.

height 60mm. Price £12

No. 99. Egyptian Kohl Pot. No. 6

Inscribed: Model of ancient Egyptian kohl pot. No. 6 Copyright.

diameter 70mm. Price £12

No. 100. Egyptian Alabaster Vase. No. 7

Inscribed: Model of ancient Egyptian alabaster vase. No. 7 Copyright

height 105mm. Price £16.50

No. 101. Egyptian Alabaster Vase. No. 8

Inscribed: Model of ancient Egyptian alabaster vase. No. 8 Copyright.

height   105mm.   Price   £16.50

No. 102. Egyptian Alabaster Bowl. No. 9

Inscribed: Model of ancient Egyptian alabaster bowl. No. 9 Copyright.

height   58mm.   Price   £12

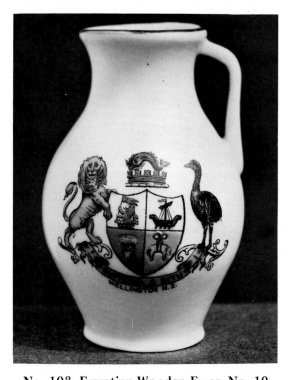

No. 103. Egyptian Wooden Ewer. No. 10

Inscribed: Model of ancient Egyptian wooden ewer. No. 10 Copyright.

height   66mm.   Price   £12

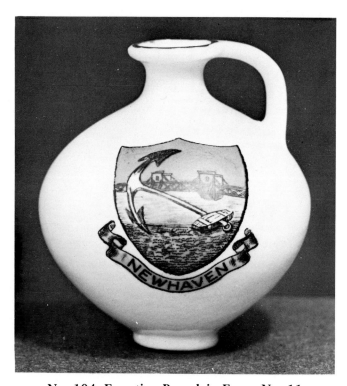

No. 104. Egyptian Porcelain Ewer. No. 11

Inscribed: Model of ancient Egyptian porcelain ewer. No. 11 Copyright.

height   58mm.   Price   £15

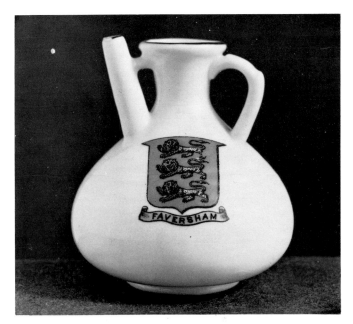

No. 105. Egyptian Porcelain Bottle. No. 16

Inscribed: Model of ancient Egyptian bottle. No. 16 Copyright.

height   68mm.   Price   £40

(No Egyptian models have been found bearing the numbers 12 to 15 inclusive).

No. 107. Ellesmere Canoe

Inscribed: Model of ancient British canoe dug out of Whattall Moss near Ellesmere in 1864. Now in Ellesmere Museum. Rd. No. 559521.

1 (a)   White   length   149mm.   Price   £47.50
2 (b)   Brown   length   149mm.   Price   £250

White models are found (seconds?) without inscription or Coat of Arms, these would bring a little over half price.

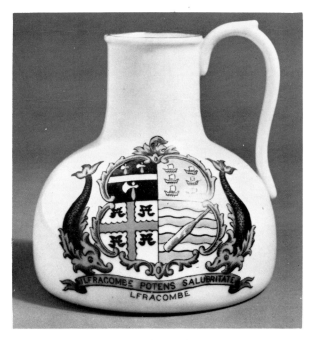

No. 106. Elizabethan Jug

Inscribed: The Elizabethan jug.

height   95mm.   Price   £12

One of the earliest of models, the production of which was thought to have been discontinued before 1900. Due to this most models seem to have lost at least part of the gilding and the colours of the arms are worn. The price given is for "mint" examples.

No. 108. English Wine Flagon

Inscribed: Model of early English wine flagon found under the foundations of Christ's Hospital, London. Rd. No. 539425.

height   90mm.   Price   £4.50

No. 109. Eton Vase

Inscribed: Model of ancient vase dredged out of the Thames near Eton. Rd. No. 539422.

height   86mm.   Price   £4

This model is identical to No. 133 Greenwich Vase.

No. 110. Exeter Goblet

Inscribed: Model of 16th century goblet found in well in Cathedral Close, Exeter.

height   130mm.   Price   £9.50

The original, considered Flemish in origin, was in Exeter Museum in 1921 and in perfect condition, and a superb example of 16th century workmanship.

No. 111. Exeter Vase

Inscribed: The Exeter vase from the original in the Museum.

(a)   height   60mm.   Price   £3.50
(b)   height 100mm.   Price   £6

No. 112. Felixstowe Cinerary Urn

Inscribed: Model of Roman cinerary urn circa A.D. 200. Found at Felixstowe from the original in the possession of S.D. Wall, Walton, Felixstowe. Rd. No. 638375.

height   47mm.   Price   £4

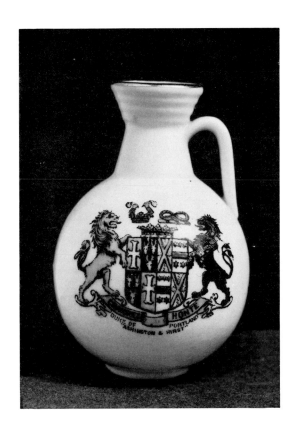

No. 113. Felixstowe Ewer

Inscribed: Model of Roman ewer found at Felixstowe, now in Ipswich Museum.

(a)	height	67mm.	Price	£4
(b)	height	110mm.	Price	£9.50

No. 114. Fenny Stratford Popper

Inscribed: Model of one of the six Fenny Stratford poppers which are fired annually on the Patronal Festival St. Martin's Day, November 11th. Founded about 1730. Copyright.

height 58mm. Price £8.50

St. Martin's Church, Fenny Stratford, was erected in 1730, on the site of an earlier building, and in this church on the 11th November St. Martin's Day is celebrated and the town fires six small cannons called "Fenny Poppers".

No. 115. Flemish Melk Pot

Inscribed: Model of old Flemish melk pot. Rd. No. 574598.

Overall length 118mm. Price £9.50

No. 116. Folkstone Ewer. (Saltwood)

Inscribed: From original found at Saltwood, now in Folkstone Museum.

height 88mm. Price £6.50

No. 118. Frazer Cuach

Inscribed: Model of Highland cuach in possession of the Frazers at Fort Augustus. Rd. No. 633433.

Overall length   104mm.   Price   £7.50

No. 117. Fountains Abbey Cup

Inscribed: Model of the Abbots cup from the original at Fountains Abbey.

    (a)   height   44mm.   Price   £3.50
    (b)   height   75mm.   Price   £7.50

Found during excavations in 1853 and in use at the time of the dissolution in the reign of Henry VIII.

No. 119. Froxfield Bowl

Inscribed: Model of Roman bronze drinking bowl found at Rudge near Froxfield, Wilts. A.D. 1725.

Diameter   72mm.   Price   £25

A very pleasing model with Coats of Arms in base of bowl. The original, deeply engraved, carries an inscription all around the side, near the top. This is clearly visible on the models.

No. 120. Gerrans Urn

Inscribed: Model of Celtic cinerary urn found at Gerrans, Cornwall.

    (a)   height   54mm.   Price   £3.50
    (b)   height   126mm.   Price   £13

The large model, which is particularly impressive, was apparently produced some years before the small one.

No. 121. Gibraltar Alcaraza

Inscribed: Model of Spanish alcaraza from Gibraltar. Rd. No. 449120.

height   68mm.   Price   £3.50

The original, a Spanish water vessel, carries a small spout where liquid was poured in, whilst opposite was a smaller spout from which the liquid was drunk. The drinking spout was not put to the lips but held some distance away. To drink in this way required considerable practice.

This model is also found incorrectly described as "Gibraltar Carafe".

Identical to No. 42 Canary Porron.

No. 122. Glastonbury Abbot Beere's Jack

Inscribed: Model of Abbot Beere's jack from carving on St. Benedict's Church, Glastonbury. Rd. No. 382436.

height   56mm.   Price   £3.50

No. 123. Glastonbury Bowl

Inscribed: Model of bowl from the ancient British Lake Village near Glastonbury.

height   36mm.   Price   £3

This model, along with No's 124 and 127, is from pieces in Glastonbury Museum, which, with many others, were found when excavating the site of the ancient British lake village at Glastonbury. The village consisted of sixty to seventy moulds, or dwellings, which were, when inhabited, surrounded by water, anything which fell in being quickly covered and concealed by the peat at the bottom. All kinds of tools, weapons and vessels were preserved, giving insight into domestic life in the Iron Age over 2000 years ago.

No. 124. Glastonbury Bronze Bowl

Inscribed: Model of bronze bowl from the ancient British Lake-village near Glastonbury.

(a)   diameter   64mm.   Price   £5.50
(b)   diameter   110mm.   Price   £20

The coats of arms on the small model is on base of inside of bowl.

The original was made of two pieces of metal riveted together. A hole in it has evidently been repaired by riveting on a small piece of metal.

No. 125. Glastonbury Roman Ewer

Inscribed: Model of ancient Roman ewer found near Glaston-bury. Rd. No. 382438.

height   71mm.   Price   £3.50

The original was found between Glastonbury and Taunton, near the Roman Road.

No. 126. Glastonbury Salt Cellar

Inscribed: Model of ancient salt cellar in Glastonbury Museum. Rd. No. 605731.

height   82mm.   Price   £8.50

No. 127. Glastonbury Vase

Inscribed: Model of vase from the ancient British Lake Village near Glastonbury.

height   45mm.   Price   £3

The model shown bears an interesting motif.

No. 128. Glen Dorgal Urn

Inscribed: Model of cinerary urn found at Glen Dorgal, now in Truro Museum. Rd. No. 594376.

height   54mm.   Price   £3.50

No. 129. Gloucester Jug

Inscribed: The Gloucester jug from original in Museum.

    (a)   height   46mm.   Price   £3.50
    (b)   height   88mm.   Price   £8.50

The original, thought to be of the Norman period, was broken in the latter part of the nineteenth century and all traces of it have been lost.

No. 130. Godalming Ewer

Inscribed: Model of ancient ewer found on Charterhouse Hill, Godalming, 31/3/1904, now in the Museum. Rd. No. 630511.

    height   55mm.   Price   £5.50

No. 131. Goodwin Sands Carafe

Inscribed: Model of ancient carafe dredged off Goodwin Sands.

    height   61mm.   Price   £3.25

No. 132. Gravesend Water Cooler

Inscribed: Model of ancient oriental water cooler found at Gravesend, from the original in Gravesend Public Library. Copyright.

    height   72mm.   Price   £10

No. 133. Greenwich Vase

Inscribed: Model of ancient vase found in Greenwich Park and of a similar one dredged out of the Thames, near Eton. Rd. No. 539422.

height   86mm.   Price   £35

This model is identical with No. 109 Eton Vase.

No. 134. Great Pyramid

Inscribed: Model of the Great Pyramid at Gizeh, near Cairo, Egypt. Rd. No. 602907.

length   96mm.   Price   £40

No. 135. Guildford Roman Vase

Inscribed: Model of Roman vase in Surrey Archeological Museum, Guildford. Rd. No. 602904.

height   63mm.   Price   £5

No. 136. Guy's Porridge Pot

Inscribed: Model of Guy's porridge pot in Warwick Castle. Rd. No. 413572.

diameter of rim   60mm.   Price   £4.50

The original, an enormous cauldron of bell metal, is still in Warwick Castle. It is capable of holding 120 gallons and weighs, with its accompanying flesh fork, over 800lbs. It is now believed to have been the garrison cooking pot.

No. 136a. Haamogi Amaui, Tonga

height   82mm.   Price   £500

No. 137. Hafod Vase

Inscribed: Model of Greek vase in Hafod Church near Devil's Bridge. Copyright.

height 76mm. Price £55

A piece we know little about, carrying a most unusual lid.

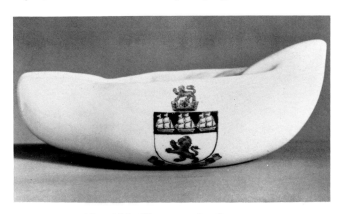

No. 138. Hamworthy Lamp

Inscribed: Model of ancient lamp found at Lake Clay Pits, Hamworthy, Poole. Rd. No. 489579.

length 100mm. Price £6

The photograph does not give quite the correct impression of the shape, as in fact it is 65mm. wide.

No. 139. Harrogate Ewer

Inscribed: Model of ancient ewer found at Aldborough Park, Harrogate. Rd. No. 639837.

height 62mm. Price £3.50

No. 140. Hastings Kettle

Inscribed: Model of ancient kettle dredged up off Hastings, 1873. In Hastings Museum.

height 51mm. Price £3.25

The original, thought to be an oil vessel and of Roman origin, was dredged up about 30 miles off Hastings covered with serpulae etc.

No. 141. Hawes British Urn

Inscribed: Model of ancient British urn found near Aysgill Force, Hawes, 1897. Rd. No. 636992.

diameter   95mm.   Price   £8.50

The model, and presumably the original, has four small holes in the side, two pairs opposite each other.

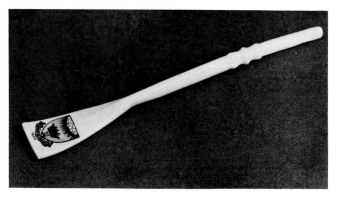

No. 142. Hawkins Henley Scull

Inscribed: Model of Hawkins Henley scull as used in the Diamonds Henley Royal Regatta. Rd. No. 636992.

length   152mm.   Price   £60

Although some collectors prefer a pair of these the model, inscribed in the singular, was issued as a single.

No. 143. Hereford Kettle

Inscribed: Model of Old Terra Cotta kettle in Hereford Museum.

(a)   height   71mm.   Price   £12.50
(b)   height   117mm.   Price   £22

Probably an oil vessel of Roman manufacture. The original was found whilst digging a well in Capuchin Lane, Hereford, 18 feet below the level of the adjoining cellar.

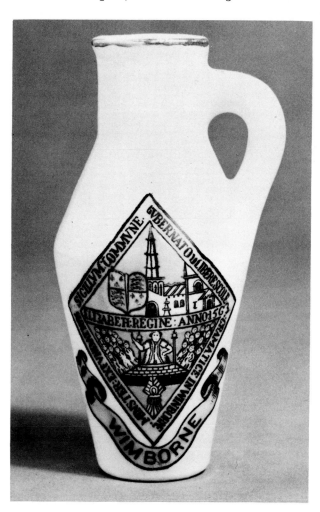

No. 144. Herne Bay Ewer

Inscribed: Model of ancient ewer found in Brickfield, Herne Bay. Rd. No. 550523.

height   78mm.   Price   £3.50

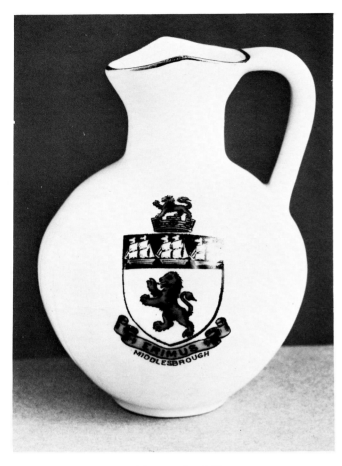

No. 145. Hertford Ewer

Inscribed: Model of ancient ewer in Hertford Museum. Rd. No. 617574.

height   69mm.   Price   £5

No. 146. Hexham Frid Stol

Inscribed: Model of the ancient frid stol in Hexham Abbey, Northumberland.

(a)	Glazed white	height	60mm.	Price	£25
(b)	Unglazed white	height	60mm.	Price	£27.50
(c)	Brown	height	60mm.	Price	£40

There are only two Frid Stols, or Sanctuary Chairs, in England, those at Hexham and Beverley, which are highly prized by historians. The chair at Hexham stood in the centre of the Sanctuary, which extended a mile around the Church. The boundaries were marked with four crosses, the sites of two, Malden Cross and White Cross, are known today. Can be found without Arms.

No. 147. Highland Cuach

Inscribed: Model of highland cuach or whiskey cup.

length   94mm.   Price   £5

No. 148. Highland Milk Crogan

Inscribed: Model of highland milk crogan made by crofters at Barvas, Isle of Lewis. Rd. No. 617576.

height   56mm.   Price   £4

No. 149. Hitchin Posset Cup

Inscribed: Model of ancient posset cup found at Hitchin. Rd. No. 521971.

height 51mm. Price £4

No. 150. Hornsea Vase (Atwick)

Inscribed: Model of Roman vase found at Atwick near Hornsea. Rd. No. 500864.

height 51mm. Price £4

No. 151. Horsham Jug

Inscribed: Model of mediaeval jug in Brighton Museum found at Horsham.

height 60mm. Price £3.25

The original, a 14th century jug, was found in an ancient kiln in West Street, Horsham, in 1867.

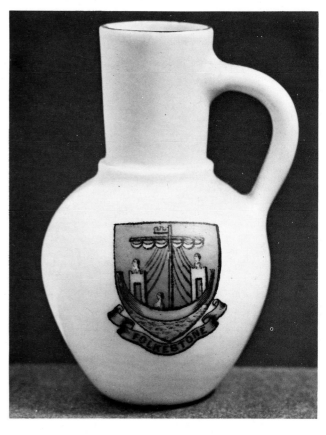

No. 152. Hunstanton Ewer

Inscribed: Model of ancient ewer found on Hunstanton Estate. Rd. No. 495669.

height 65mm. Price £3.50

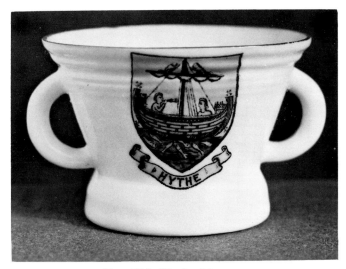

No. 153. Hythe Mortar

Inscribed: Model of Cromwellian mortar found at Hythe. Rd. No. 590750.

height 38mm. Price £4.50

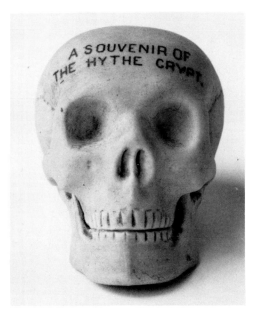

No. 154. Hythe Crypt Skull

Inscribed: A souvenir of the Hythe Crypt.

height approx. 35mm. Price £30

This model is only found in a pale yellow colour.

No. 155. Ilkley Ewer

Inscribed: Model of Roman Ewer in Ilkley Museum. Rd. No. 489582.

(a) height 60mm. Price £3.50
(b) height 132mm. Price £12

No. 156. Ipswich Ancient Ewer

Inscribed: Model of ancient ewer dug up in Ipswich now in museum. Rd. No. 553188.

height 60mm. Price £3.75

No. 157. Ipswich Roman Ewer

Inscribed: Model of Roman ewer dug up in Ipswich now in museum.

height 98mm. Price £12

No. 158. Irish Bronze Pot

Inscribed: Model of ancient Irish bronze pot.

(a)	height	44mm.	Price	£3.25
(b)	height	71mm.	Price	£5.50

No. 159. Irish Mather

Inscribed: Model of Irish mather or wooden drinking cup in Dorset County Museum.

(a)	height	74mm.	Price	£5.50
(b)	height	148mm.	Price	£27.50

The large size carries either two, three, or four coats of arms on one side and a verse on the other.

No. 160. Irish Wooden Noggin

Inscribed: Model of ancient Irish wooden noggin. Rd. No. 489580.

height 63mm. Price £5

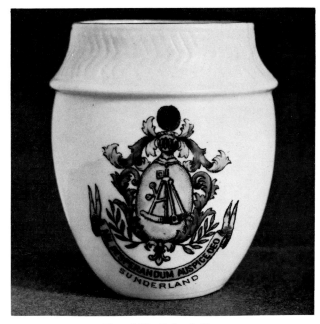

No. 161. Itford Urn

Inscribed: Model of British urn found at Itford near Lewes.
Rd. No. 573577.

(a)	height	66mm.	Price	£4
(b)	height	97mm.	Price	£12.50

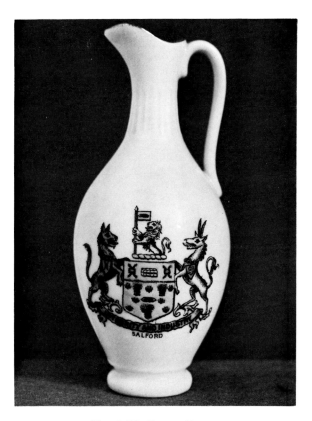

No. 162. Japan Ewer

Inscribed: The Japan ewer.

(a)	height	90mm.	Price	£5
(b)	height	196mm.	Price	£14

No. 163. Kendal Jug

Inscribed: Model of jug in Kendal Museum dated 1602.

(a)	height	84mm.	Price	£4
(b)	height	146mm.	Price	£18.50

The original, of stoneware, and similar to Flemish Ware, was said to have belonged to Kendal Castle and to have had six coats of arms of English Cities and Sees embossed around it, with the date 1602.

No. 164. Kettering Urn

Inscribed: Model of ancient urn found at Kettering now in Northampton Museum. Rd. No. 543008.

height	43mm.	Price	£3.50

63

No. 165. Kininmonth Moss Pot

Inscribed: Model of ancient moss pot dug out of Kininmonth Moss near Old Dear in 1855 Copyright.

height   49mm.   Price   £10

No. 166. Lancaster Jug

Inscribed: Model of ancient jug in Lancaster Museum. Rd. No. 500863.

height   68mm.   Price   £3.50

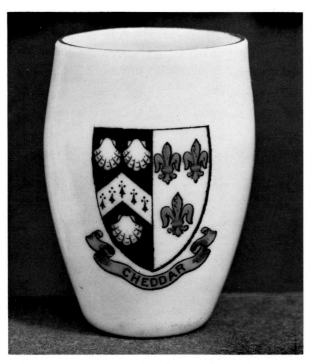

No. 167. Lanlawren Urn

Inscribed: Model of Celtic sepulchral urn, found at Lanlawren, Cornwall.

(a)   height   53mm.   Price   £3.25
(b)   height   106mm.   Price   £12

No. 168. Las Palmas Ancient Jarra

Inscribed: Model of ancient jarra in museum Las Palmas Grand Canary. Rd. No. 572204.

height   53mm.   Price   £5.50

No. 169. Las Palmas Covered Jarra

Inscribed: Model of ancient covered jarra in Museum Las Palmas Grand Canary. Rd. No. 572205.

height
with lid 58mm. Price £6.50

This model is of virtually no value without lid.

No. 170. Las Palmas Earthen Jar

Inscribed: Model of ancient earthen jar in Museum Las Palmas Grand Canary. Rd. No. 610010.

height 58mm. Price £4.50

No. 171. Laxey Urn

Inscribed: Model of ancient urn found at Gretch-Veg near Laxey I.O.M. Rd. No. 489581.

(a) diameter 55mm. Price £4
(b) diameter 55mm. Price £4

(a) has the Coat of Arms on the side as shown in illustration.
(b) has the Arms on the inside base of the bowl and is ornamented all round.

No. 172. Leek Urn

Inscribed: Model of British urn found at Hen Cloud nr. Leek. Rd. No. 500865.

height 63mm. Price £4

No. 173. Leicester Tyg

Inscribed: Model of Tyg found in Highcross Street 1867 now in Leicester Museum. Rd. No. 495670.

height   59mm.   Price   £5

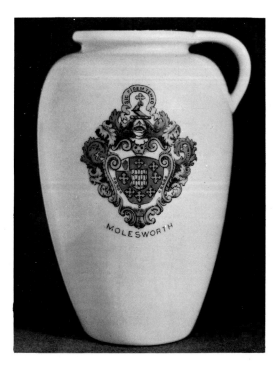

No. 174. Leiston Pitcher

Inscribed: Model of pitcher in Ipswich Museum found at Leiston Abbey.

(a)   height   56mm.   Price   £3.50
(b)   height   107mm.   Price   £10

No. 175. Letchworth Carinated Vase

Inscribed: Model of Roman carinated vase 120-140 A.D. in Letchworth Museum. Copyright.

height   60mm.   Price   £60

No. 176. Letchworth Celtic Urn

Inscribed: Model of late Celtic cinerary urn in Letchworth Museum found in 1912 Copyright.

height   97mm.   Price   £22.50

No. 177. Lewes Vase
Inscribed: Model of Roman vase in Lewes Castle.

height   35mm.   Price   £3

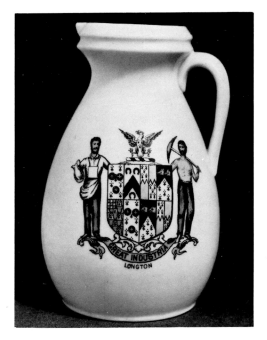

No. 178. Lichfield Jug
Inscribed: Model of ancient jug dug out of the foundations of Lichfield Museum.

(a)	height	57mm.	Price	£3.25
(b)	height	120mm.	Price	£10

The original, according to the museum label, was found some 20 feet below the surface in 1859.

No. 179. Lincoln Jack
Inscribed: Model of Lincoln Jack – this jack was the gift of Alderman Bullen to the company of ringers.

(a)		height	65mm.	Price	£3.50
(b)		height	147mm.	Price	£14.50
(c)	black	height	147mm.	Price	£750

Only one of (c) is known to the author and it is considered to be authentic.

No. 180. Lincoln Vase
Inscribed: Model of Lincoln vase from original at Museum.

(a)	height	63mm.	Price	£3.50
(b)	height	88mm.	Price	£5.50

No. 181. Littlehampton Ewer

Inscribed: Model of Roman ewer found when pulling down houses in Arundel Road, Littlehampton. Rd. No. 521977.

height   73mm.   Price   £4

No. 182. Llandudno Vase (Gogarth)

Inscribed: Model of ancient vase found at Gogarth, Marine Drive Llandudno. Copyright.

height   84mm.   Price   £7.50

No. 183. Llandudno Vase. (Little Orme)

Inscribed: Model of Roman vase found on the Little Orme, Llandudno 17/Dec/19. Copyright.

height   82mm.   Price   £8.50

No. 184. Lobster Trap

Inscribed: Model of lobster trap.

(a)   diameter of base   67mm.   Price   £7.50
(b)   diameter of base   118mm.   Price   £18

Models inscribed "Manx" or "Channel Islands" Lobster Traps are known. These would bring double the normal price.

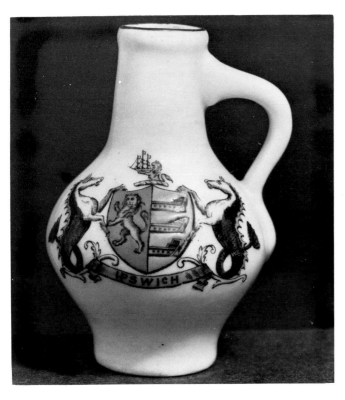

No. 185. Looe Ewer

Inscribed: Model of ancient ewer in St. Nicholas Church Looe. Rd. No. 450629.

height   65mm.   Price   £3.50

The original, thought to be 15th Century, was found bricked up in a niche in the Church. Considered to be the vessel that held the oil with which the sick were anointed.

No. 186. Louth Ancient Ewer

Inscribed: Model of ancient ewer found at Louth. Rd. No. 449119.

(a)   height   49mm.   Price   £3.50
(b)   height   110mm.   Price   £16.50

No. 187. Ludlow Sack Bottle

Inscribed: Model of sack bottle dug up in castle moat, Ludlow, now in Ludlow Museum.

height   75mm.   Price   £7.50

The original, a dark green stone vessel, made of flint, was possibly a relic of the days when Charles II, then the Prince of Wales, held court in Ludlow.

No. 188. Luton Costrel

Inscribed: Model of "costrell" or farm labourers water bottle, circa 16th century. Made of local clay at St. Mary's Pottery, Skimpot. Dug up on the site of the London & County Bank, Luton, May 1898. Rd. No. 630308.

height   65mm.   Price   £7.50

No. 189. Lyme Regis Ammonite

Inscribed: Model of Lyme Regis ammonite. Rd. No. 513063.

height   73mm.   Price   £20

The original, which was found in the cliffs at Lyme Regis, was considered the most perfect ammonite found. Despite this, the model is identical with No. 291 Whitby Ammonite. A little of Goss's harmless dishonesty.

No. 190. Madeira Bullock Car

Inscribed: Model of Madeira Bullock Car. Copyright.

height   55mm.   Price   £500

This model is extremely rare and the only specimen known is damaged. The price quoted is for a model in perfect condition. Until an undamaged piece is discovered the damaged one has a price which would not apply if even one perfect example was known.

No. 191. Maidstone Ewer

Inscribed: Model of Roman ewer, from the original in Maidstone Museum, Maidstone.

(a)	height	82mm.	Price	£4.50
(b)	height	132mm.	Price	£8.50

No. 192. Maltese Carafe

Inscribed: Model of Maltese carafe. Rd. No. 539424.

height   105mm.   Price   £10

No. 193. Maltese Double-Mouthed Vase

Inscribed: Model of double-mouthed vase of bronze age period, from Tarxien Sanctuary.

height   60mm.   Price   £18

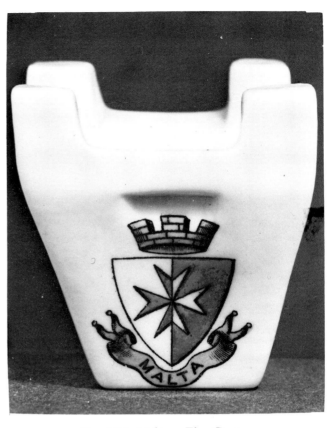

No. 194. Maltese Fire Grate

Inscribed: Model of Maltese fire grate.

height   52mm.   Price   £10

No. 195. Maltese Funeral Urn

Inscribed: Model of Maltese funereal urn (circa 600 B.C.) found in Rock Tombs, Malta. Rd. No. 559525.

height   61mm.   Price   £4

No. 196. Maltese Twin Vase

Inscribed: Model of Maltese twin vase from Tarxien Sanctuary. Bronze age period.

height   50mm.   Price   £30

No. 197. Maltese Two-Wick Lamp

Inscribed: Model of Maltese two-wick lamp (circa 600 B.C.) found in Rock Tombs, Malta. Rd. No. 562738.

length 81mm. Price £7.50

No. 198. Maltese Vase a Canard

Inscribed: Model of Maltese vase a canard of bronze age period from Tarxien Sanctuary.

height 45mm. Price £7.50

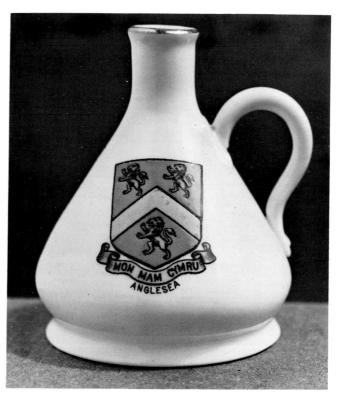

No. 199. Manx Pot

Inscribed: Model of old manx pot at Peel. Rd. No. 390789.

height 49mm. Price £4

This model is identical with No. 165 Kininmonth Moss Pot.

No. 200. Manx Spirit Measure

Inscribed: Model of ancient Manx spirit measure. Rd. No. 578695.

height 68mm. Price £5

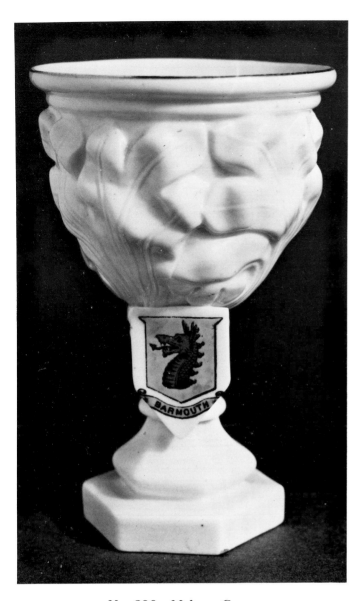

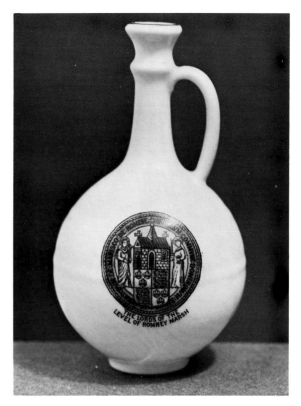

No. 201. Minster Ewer

Inscribed: Model of ancient ewer found at Minster, Thanet. Copyright.

height   88mm.   Price   £9.50

No. 200a. Melrose Cup

Inscribed: The Melrose Cup

height   128mm.   Price   £35

No. 200b. Maple Leaf of Canada

height   118mm.   Price   £80

Right: No. 202. Minster Urn

Inscribed: Model of ancient urn found at Minster, Kent. Copyright:

height   65mm.   Price   £7.50

No. 203. Monmouth Masks

Inscribed: Model of mask from Geoffrey of Monmouth's study at Monmouth.

1	(a)	The "Knight"	White	Price	£225
	(b)	The "Knight"	Brown	Price	£300
2	(a)	The "Angel"	White	Not now believed to exist	
	(b)	The "Angel"	Brown	Not now believed to exist	
3	(a)	The "Miller"	White	Price	£225
	(b)	The "Miller"	Brown	Price	£300

The illustration shows Knight and Miller.

No. 204. Mons Meg

Inscribed: Model of "Mons Meg" Edinburgh Castle. Rd. No. 605732.

length 122mm. Price £25

The original, probably forged in Galloway around 1455, could fire a 5cwt. stone cannon-ball about one and a half miles.

No. 205. Munich Beer Seidel

Inscribed: Model of Munich beer seidel.

height 52mm. Price £25

A small but elusive piece.

No. 206. Musselburgh Urn

Inscribed: Model of ancient urn found in Kirkpark Musselburgh N.B. Rd. No. 448431.

height   51mm.   Price   £3

The model illustrated shows a military emblem, of which there are many examples. They are much sought after.

No. 207. Newbury Leather Bottle

Inscribed: Model of leather bottle found on battle-field of Newbury. 1644. Now in Museum.

(a)	height	58mm.	Price	£3.25
(b)	height	113mm.	Price	£7.50

No. 208. Newcastle Cup

Inscribed: Model of an ancient black-&-brown cup dug up at the south side of Red Lion Square, Newcastle, Staffs. in 1882: now in the possession of Messrs. Chapman & Snape.

height   70mm.   Price   £8.50

No. 209. Newcastle Jug

Inscribed: Model of Roman jug in the museum Newcastle on Tyne. Rd. No. 392069.

height   63mm.   Price   £3.25

No. 210. Norwegian Bucket

Inscribed: Model of Norwegian bucket. Rd. No. 599332.

height   58mm.   Price   £7.50

No. 212. Norwegian Horse-headed Beer Bowl

Inscribed: Model of Norwegian horse-shaped beer bowl. Rd. No. 526383.

length   115mm.   Price   £11

No. 211. Norwegian Dragon Beer Bowl

Inscribed: Model of Norwegian dragon shaped beer bowl. Rd. No. 526382.

length   155mm.   Price   £12.50

No. 213. Norwich Urn

Inscribed: Model of the Norwich urn from the original in the museum.

(a)	height	49mm.	Price	£3.25
(b)	height	62mm.	Price	£4.25
(c)	height	88mm.	Price	£8

The original, with several other pieces, was found during excavations in the Market Place, Norwich.

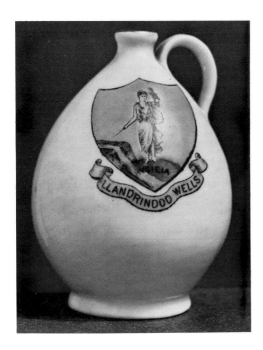

No. 214. Nottingham Ewer

Inscribed: Model of ancient ewer found during excavations top of Long Stairs High Pavement, Nottingham. Now in Castle Museum. Rd. No. 472576.

height   63mm.   Price   £3.50

No. 215. Nottingham Urn

Inscribed: Model of ancient urn found during excavations in Nottingham 1897. Now in Castle Museum. Rd. No. 472577.

height   40mm.   Price   £3.25

No. 216. Orkney Craisie

Inscribed: Model of Orkney Craisie. Rd. No. 559522.

height   80mm.   Price   £15

A beautiful model of the basket used in the Orkney Islands. The description and mark are inside the basket.

No. 217. Ostend Bottle

Inscribed: Model of Flemish bottle Ostend Museum. Rd. No. 495673.

height   65mm.   Price   £4

No. 218. Ostend Tobacco Jar

Inscribed: Model of Flemish tobacco jar in Liebaert Museum at Ostend. Rd. No. 495674.

height   54mm.   Price   £3.25

No. 219. Ostend Vase

Inscribed: Model of Ostend vase A.D. 1617, found inside a fishing smack in the Fisherman's Dock at Ostend. Now in Ostend Museum. Rd. No. 495672.

height   57mm.   Price   £3.25

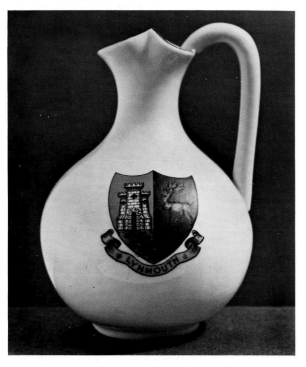

No. 220. Oxford Ewer

Inscribed: The Oxford Ewer from the original in the Ashmolean Museum, found at Exeter Coll.

(a)   height   73mm.   Price   £3.50
(b)   height   122mm.   Price   £8.50

No. 221. Oxford Jug

Inscribed: The Oxford Jug from the original in the Ashmolean Museum, found at Trinity Coll.

height   173mm.   Price   £16

One of the earliest models often carrying both the impressed and printed marks.

No. 222. Painswick Pot

Inscribed: Model of Roman pot found at Ifold Villa Painswick 1902. Rd. No. 500869.

height   50mm.   Price   £3

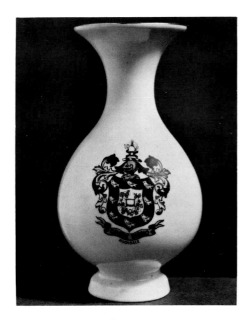

No. 223. Panama Vase

Inscribed: Panama Vase. Rd. No. 639532.

height   128mm.   Price   £25

No. 224. Penmaenmawr Urn

Inscribed: Model of ancient urn found at Penmaenmawr.

height   45mm.   Price   £3.25

The original, found in Penmaenmawr in 1890, was thought to be of very early date, being fashioned by hand and not thrown on a wheel.

No. 225. Perth Coronation Chair

Inscribed: Model of the Coronation Chair in Westminster Abbey. Rd. No. 578694. The chair contains the ancient stone on which the Kings and Queens of Scotland were formerly crowned at Scone, Perthshire.

(a)   Stone under seat white
       height   88mm.   Price   £75
(b)   Stone under seat brown
       height   88mm.   Price   £125

Identical to No. 76 Coronation Chair apart from the fact that it carries the extra inscription after the Registered Number. Always carries the Perth Coats of Arms.

No. 226. Peterborough Tripod

Inscribed: Model of bronze Roman tripod in Peterborough Museum found at Whittlesey Mere.

height   47mm.   Price   £6.50

This model is identical in design to No. 484. Witch's Cauldron.

No. 227. Pine Cone

Inscribed: Model of Pine Cone. Rd. No. 559524.

height   90mm.   Price   £7.50

Often called the 'Bournemouth Pine Cone' and the correct Coats of Arms for this piece is Bournemouth.

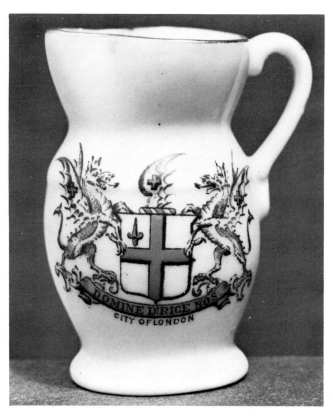

No. 228. Plymouth Jug

Inscribed: Model of old Spanish jug dredged up near Eddystone now in Athenaeum Plymouth.

height   55mm.   Price   £3.25

The original, glazed and crudely decorated in brown, yellow and blue, was dredged up by fishermen.

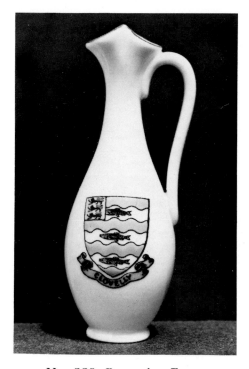

No. 229. Pompeian Ewer

Inscribed: Model of Pompeian Ewer (The large size does not normally carry an inscription).

(a)   height   88mm.   Price   £5
(b)   height   206mm.   Price   £16.50

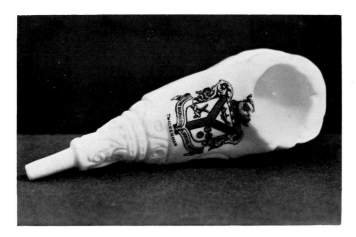

No. 230. Pope's Pipe

Inscribed: Model of antique pipe found among the debris of Pope's house at Twickenham.

length 118mm. Price £25

No. 231. Portland Vase

(a) Inscribed: Model of the Portland Vase in the British Museum.
(b) Carries a commemorative inscription marking the centenary of the death of Josiah Wedgwood.

(a)	height	51mm.	Price	£3.50
(b)	height	51mm.	Price	£25

See also No. 385.

No. 232. Preston Bushel Measure

Inscribed: Model of the old bushel measure made for Preston in 1670 and used by the mayor and clerk of the markets under the old charters granted to the town.

diameter 58mm. Price £75

The raised inscription around the side reads 'For Preston in the County of Lancashire 1670'.

No. 233. Queen Charlotte's Kettle

Inscribed: Model of Queen Charlotte's Windsor favourite now in William H. Goss's Collection.

height 170mm. Price £100

Incomplete without lid.

The original apparently belonged to a lady in Windsor and was admired by the Queen, who was a frequent visitor.

No. 234. Queen Phillipa's Record Chest

Inscribed: Model of Queen Phillipa's record chest found in Knaresborough Castle. Rd. No. 643868.

(a)	length	80mm.	Price	£27.50
(b)	length	94mm.	Price	£27.50

No. 235 Ramsgate Ewer

Inscribed: Model of Romano British 1st century ewer found at Ramsgate. 794 Copyright.

height   47mm.   Price   £10

No. 236 Ramsgate Jug

Inscribed: Model of Romano-British 1st century jug found at Ramsgate 795 Copyright.

height   70mm.   Price   £12.50

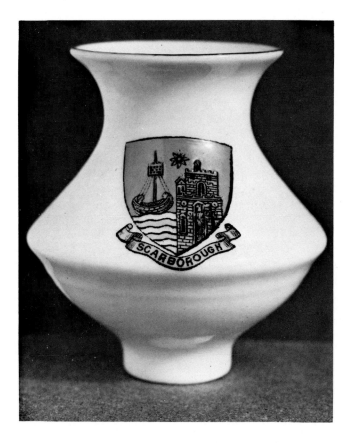

No. 237. Ramsgate Urn

Inscribed: Model of ancient urn found at Ramsgate 787 Copyright.

height   75mm.   Price   £8

No. 238. Rayleigh Cooking Pot

Inscribed: Model of ancient cooking pot found at Rayleigh Castle Essex. Rd. No. 602903.

height 33mm. Price £3.25

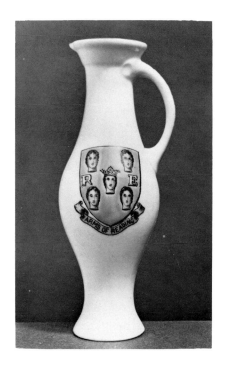

No. 239. Reading Jug

Inscribed: Model of 15th century jug dug up in Minster St. Reading. Now in museum.

(a) height 82mm. Price £3.25
(b) height 145mm. Price £7.50

No. 240. Reading Urn

Inscribed: Model of Roman urn from Silchester in Reading Museum. Rd. No. 573577.

height 50mm. Price £3.25

No. 241. Reading Vase

Inscribed: Model of vase from Silchester in Reading Museum.

height 50mm. Price £3.25

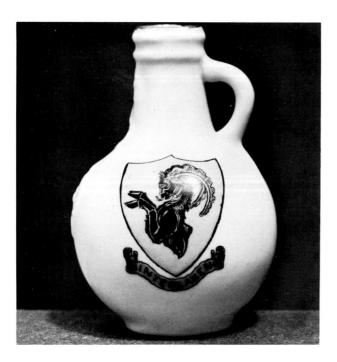

No. 242. Rochester Ballarmine

Inscribed: Model of Bellarmine jug 17th century found in Rochester. Rd. No. 403421.

height   65mm.   Price   £3.50

This model is identical to No. 78 Cuckfield Bellarmine.

No. 243. Roman Mortarium

Inscribed: Model of ancient Roman mortarium.

diameter   95mm.   Price   £30

This model is also found un-named and without Coat of Arms.

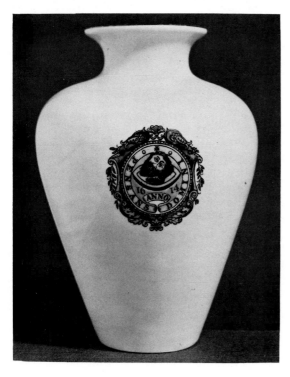

No. 244. Roman Vase 783

Inscribed: The Roman Vase 783 Copyright.

height   160mm.   Price   £50

No. 245. Romsey Bushel

Inscribed: Model of ancient Romsey bushel in the possession of the Corporation. Rd. No. 489663.

diameter   68mm.   Price   £7.50

The arms are on the inside base.

No. 246. Rye Cannon Ball

Inscribed: Model of cannon ball excavated at Landgate, Rye 1907. This ball was probably fired by the French who twice burnt Rye to the ground (1377 & 1448)

(a) Brown, without pedestal   height   68mm.   Price £30
(b) Brown, with white pedestal height   106mm.   Price £85

No. 247. St. Albans Cooking Pot

Inscribed: Model of ancient cooking pot in St. Albans Museum. Rd. No. 633430.

        height   58mm.   Price   £5

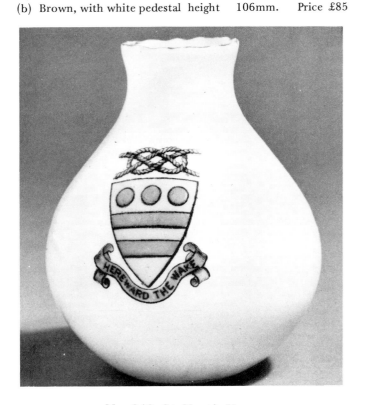

No. 248. St. Neot's Urn

Inscribed: Model of ancient urn found 1816 near St. Neot's, Hunts. Rd. No. 413576.

        height   63mm.   Price   £3.75

No. 249. Salisbury Kettle

Inscribed: Model of old kettle in Salisbury Museum.

(a)   height   80mm.   Price   £7.50
(b)   height   135mm.   Price   £10

No. 250. Salisbury Leather Jack

Inscribed: Model of the Royal Salisbury jack from original in museum.

    (a)   height   44mm.   Price   £3.50
    (b)   height   133mm.   Price   £12.50

The emblem as shown on illustration is considered to be more correct than arms for this piece.

No. 251. Salisbury Gill

Inscribed: The Salisbury leather gill from original in museum.

    height   75mm.   Price   £6.50

This model has a handle not shown in illustration.
The inscription on sides reads 'R.S.M.' on the left, '1658' on right.

No. 252. Scarborough Kettle

Inscribed: Model of the Scarboro kettle found near ancient pottery, north side.

    (a)   height   65mm.   Price   £6.50
    (b)   height   90mm.   Price   £10

No. 253. Scarborough Jug

Inscribed: Model of jug about 600 years old found in the ancient moat of Scarborough.

    (a)   height   45mm.   Price   £3.50
    (b)   height   67mm.   Price   £5.50

The original was found in the old moat at the back of Huntress Row and thought to be of Norman origin.

No. 254. Seaford Urn

Inscribed: Model of Roman urn found at Seaford 1825.

height   48mm.   Price   £4

This was reputedly modelled from an illustration in Banks and Turner's "Seaford, Past and Present". The original is reported to have been found in a grave near Lyon Place, Seaford, the site of a Romano-British Cemetery. It is rather a squat little model, being some 70mm. in diameter.

No. 255. Shakespeare's Jug

Inscribed either on neck or side: Model of jug of William Shakespeare.

(a)	height	50mm.	Price	£5
(b)	height	73mm.	Price	£12
(c)	height	88mm.	Price	£17.50

As shown in the illustration the name is a facsimile of the poet's signature.

No. 256. Shepherds Crown Sea Urchin

Inscribed: Model of fossil sea urchin found on the downs at Steyning, locally known as Shepherds Crowns. Copyright.

height   50mm.   Price   £20

This piece was listed in 1921 as being in preparation and the price was given as 2/-.

No. 257. Shrewsbury Ewer

Inscribed: Model of ewer, found in the ancient Roman city of Uriconium, Nr Shrewsbury.

height   97mm.   Price   £12.50

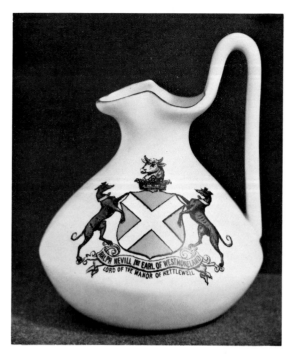

No. 258. Shrewsbury Romano-Salopian Ewer

Inscribed: Model of Romano-Salopian ewer found at Uriconium. Now in Shrewsbury Museum.

height   68mm.   Price   £3.75

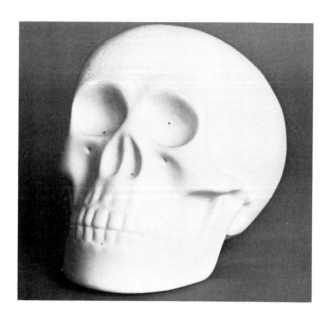

No. 259. Simon of Sudbury's Skull

Inscription: Skull of St. Simon of Sudbury.

height   72mm.   Price   £200

The first example of this extremely scarce piece has only recently come to light. It would appear to be similar to the other skulls that the firm made, but in this case it is in white Parian.

No. 260. Southampton Pipkin

Inscribed: Model of ancient pipkin dug up at N.P. Bank Southampton.

(a)	height	55mm.	Price	£3.25
(b)	height	76mm.	Price	£12.50
(c)	height	100mm.	Price	£12.50

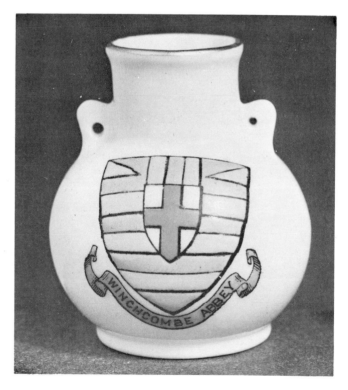

No. 261. Southport Vase

Inscribed: Model of vase at Botanic Gardens Southport. Rd. No. 403423.

height   50mm.   Price   £3.25

No. 262 Southwold Gun

Reputed inscription: Model of ancient gun washed out of Gun Hill Cliff, Southwold, now in the Town Hall.

approximate length   100mm.   Price   £200

No. 263. Southwold Jar

Inscribed: Model of ancient jar washed out of cliff near Southwold, now in town hall.

(a)   height   85mm.   Price   £3.50
(b)   height   138mm.   Price   £10

No. 264. Stirling Pint Measure

Inscribed: Model of the Stirling pint measure. One of the ancient standard measures of Scotland deposited in Stirling by Act of Parliament 1457. Rd. No. 543012.

height   61mm.   Price   £5.50

No. 265 Stockport Plague Stone

Inscribed: Model of plague stone found during excavations in Stockport market place. Original now in Vernon Park Museum, Stockport. The hollow was filled with vinegar, and when food etc. was brought into the town, the money was placed in the vinegar to prevent infection.

height   75mm.   Price   £10

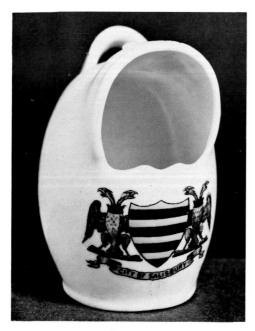

No. 266. Stockton Salt Pot

Inscribed: Model of ancient salt pot found in bed of river at Stockton-on-Tees. Rd. No. 406301.

height 73mm. Price £4.50

The original, probably 17th century, was dark brown in colour with incised white decoration, about 9ins. high with aperture large enough for the hand.

No. 267. Sunderland Bottle

Inscribed: Model of ancient bottle in Sunderland Museum. Rd. No. 392068.

length 58mm. Price £3.25

The original was considered to be of Peruvian origin.

No. 268. Swindon Vase

Inscribed: Model of vase dug up near Swindon.

(a) height 56mm. Price £3.25
(b) height 108mm. Price £7.50

No. 269. Swiss Cow Bell

Inscribed: Model of old Swiss cow bell.

(a) height 54mm. Price £7.50
(b) height 74mm. Price £8.50

Only complete when porcelain clapper is hung inside.

No. 271. Swiss Milk Pot

Inscribed: Model of old Swiss milk pot. Rd. No. 500867.

height, including lid   82mm.   Price   £10

Of little value without lid.

No. 270. Swiss Milk Bucket

Inscribed: Model of Swiss milk bucket. Rd. No. 526385.

(a)   height   55mm.   Price   £5.50
(b)   height   88mm.   Price   £7.50

No. 273. Tewkesbury Urn

Inscribed: Model of Saxon urn found at the Tolsey, Tewkesbury. Rd. No. 411451.

height   45mm.   Price   £3.25

The model illustrated carries the emblem of heather on one side and a thistle on the other.

No. 272. Swiss Vinegar Bottle

Inscribed: Model of old Swiss vinegar bottle. Rd. No. 496832.

length   75mm.   Price   £4.50

No. 274. Tintern Water Bottle

Inscribed: Model of ancient water bottle found during excavations for bridge at Brockweir, Tintern. 1907. Rd. No. 626750.

height 76mm. Price £4.50

Faithful reproduction of original, even to the broken handle.

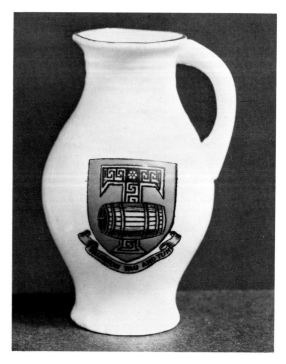

No. 275. Tonbridge Ewer

Inscribed: Model of Roman ewer found in Eastcheap London now in Tonbridge Museum. Rd. No. 599334.

height 63mm. Price £3.50

No. 276. Tresco Beacon

Inscribed: Model of the old brazier at Tresco formerly the beacon light at St. Agnes, Isles of Scilly. Rd. No. 589292.

height 69mm. Price £10

Included by many in their lighthouse collection, with some justification.

No. 277. Tresvannack Urn

Inscribed: Model of ancient urn found at Tresvannack, St. Paul, Cornwall. Rd. No. 594378.

height 55mm. Price £5

No. 277a. Tuscan Vase

Inscribed: The Tuscan vase. 783 Copyright.
height approx.   150mm.   Price   £100

No. 278. Tyg

Inscribed: Model of ancient tyg.

(a)	One-handled	height	65mm.	Price	£3.50
(b)	Two-handled	height	65mm.	Price	£3.50

No. 279. Walden Abbey Urn

Inscribed: Model of covered urn found near site of Walden Abbey in 1878.

(a)	height to top of lid	70mm.	Price	£10
(b)	height to top of lid	120mm.	Price	£15

Practically valueless without 'Mummy's head' lid.

No. 280. Walmer Roman Vase

Inscribed: Model of Roman vase. Found at Walmer Lodge. Rd. No. 382437.

height   65mm.   Price   £3.25

The original, of green glass, when found was full of burnt bones, thought to be the remains of a Roman General.

No. 281. Wareham Bottle

Inscribed: Model of Roman Bottle found at Wareham. Rd. No. 500866.

height   67mm.   Price   £3.50

No. 282. Waterlooville Bottle

Inscribed: Model of army water bottle used at the Battle of Waterloo, Waterlooville.

When the troops came back after "Waterloo" their first camp was at this place which thus obtained its name.

The original water bottle which is of oak, bound with brass, was left behind by one of the soldiers. Rd. No. 638373.

height   83mm.   Price   £8.50

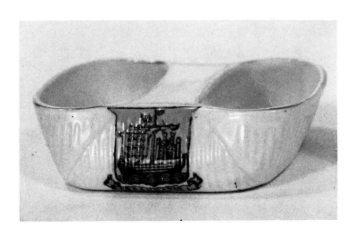

No. 283. Welsh Coracle

Inscribed: Model of Welsh Coracle. Survival of ancient British wicker and hide boats.

length   77mm.   Price   £12.50

No. 284. Welsh Crochon

Inscribed: Model of ancient Welsh bronze crochon, about A.D. 400, dug up at Caerhun Conovium, in collection of W.H. Goss.

(a)	diameter of bowl	62mm.	Price	£4.50
(b)	diameter of bowl	70mm.	Price	£6.50
(c)	diameter of bowl	87mm.	Price	£12.50
(d)	diameter of bowl	117mm.	Price	£22.50

No. 285. Welsh Hat

Inscribed: Model of hat formerly worn by women in Wales.

diameter of brim   74mm.   Price   £7.50

Can be found with the longest Welsh place name round the brim. Value £40.

No. 286. Welsh Jack

Inscribed: Model of Welsh Jack.

height including lid   120mm.   Price   £12

Incomplete and practically worthless without lid.

No. 287. Welsh Milk Can

Inscribed: Model of old Welsh milk can.

(a)	height, with lid	70mm.	Price	£5.50
(b)	height, with lid	108mm.	Price	£8.50
(c)	height, with lid	140mm.	Price	£12.50

Of little value without lid.

Identical in design to No. 53. Channel Islands Milk Can.

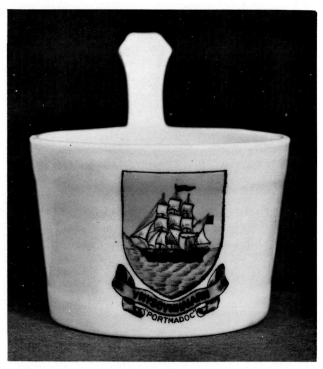

No. 288. Welsh Picyn

Inscribed: Model of Welsh picyn or porridge bowl. Rd. No. 543010.

height to top of handle   62mm.   Price   £7

No. 289. Wensleydale Jack

Inscribed: Model of Wensleydale Jack date about 1500 in Hornes Museum Leyburn. Rd. No. 521972.

height   67mm.   Price   £3.50

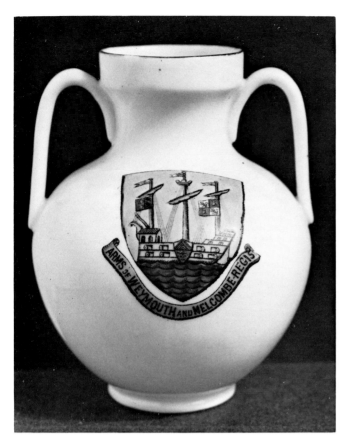

No. 290. Weymouth Vase

Inscribed: Model of Roman vase found at Jordon Hill, Weymouth, now in Dorset Museum.

(a)	height	55mm.	Price	£3.50
(b)	height	92mm.	Price	£7.50

No. 291. Whitby Ammonite

Inscribed: Model of the Whitby Ammonite. Rd. No. 513063.

height   73mm.   Price   £16.50

Identical to No. 189. Lyme Regis Ammonite.

No. 292. Whitby Pillion Stone

Inscribed: Model of old pillion stone Flowergate, Whitby. Rd. No. 641311.

length   72mm.   Price   £16.50

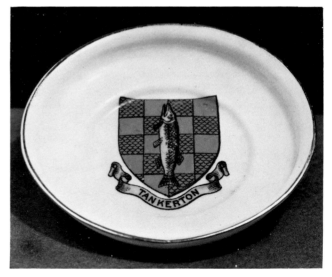

No. 293. Whitstable Tray

Inscribed: Model of Roman patera about 1600 years old dredged up off Whitstable.

diameter   88mm.   Price   £6.50

No. 294. Winchester Bushel

Inscribed: Reduced model of Winchester bushel.

(a)	height	38mm.	Price	£120
(b)	height	50mm.	Price	£125
(c)	height	58mm.	Price	£225

No. 295. Winchester Jack

Inscribed: Model of the black Jack at Winchester College (see footnote).

(a)	height	32mm.	Price	£16.50
(b)	height	46mm.	Price	£3.50
(c)	height	85mm.	Price	£10
(d)	height	120mm.	Price	£22.50

The illustration shows the Trusty Servant Emblem, which would double the value of the piece.

On pieces showing the Trusty Servant, three largest sizes only, an extra inscription is give viz. 'A piece of Antiquity painted on the wall adjoining to the kitchen of Winchester College'. They also carry the verse about the Trusty Servant on the back.

No. 296. Winchester Quart

Inscribed: Model of Winchester Quart Temp. Q. Elizabeth.

height   92mm.   Price   £225

This model does not carry coats of arms.

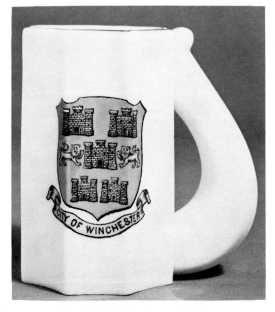

No. 297. Winchester Pot

Inscribed: Model of pot dug up at George Hotel, Winchester.

height   74mm.   Price   £8.50

No. 298. Winchester Warden's Horn

Inscribed: Warden's Horn, Winchester Castle, A.D. 1300.

(a)	with stand	length	152mm.	Price	£350
(b)	without stand length		152mm.	Price	£200

This model does not carry a Coat of Arms.

No. 300. Winsford Salt Lump

Inscribed: Model of salt lump as made at Winsford, Cheshire.

height   80mm.   Price   £45

This model is identical in design to No. 56 Cheshire Salt Block.

No. 299. Windsor Urn

Inscribed: Urn found at Old Windsor, from original in museum.

(a)	height	44mm.	Price	£3.25
(b)	height	85mm.	Price	£6.50

No. 301. Wisbech Jug

Inscribed: Model of ancient jug found in Wisbech River, 1848, in museum.

height   82mm.   Price   £14

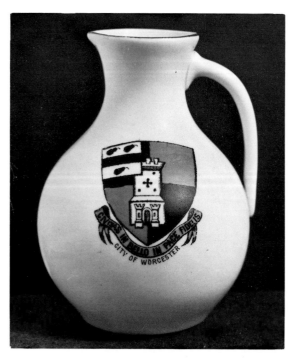

No. 302. Worcester Jug

Inscribed: The Worcester jug from the original in the museum, found at Castle Hill.

(a)	height	62mm.	Price	£4.50
(b)	height	100mm.	Price	£7.50

No. 303. Wymondham Jar

Inscribed: Model of ancient jar found in the Abbey ruins Wymondham. Rd. No. 617572.

height 61mm. Price £5

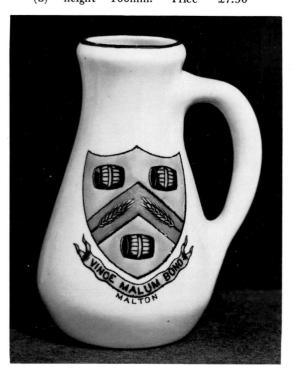

No. 304. Yarmouth Ewer

Inscribed: Model of early English Ewer dredged up in River Yare now in Yarmouth Museum. Rd. No. 495671.

height 62mm. Price £3.50

No. 305. Yarmouth Jug

Inscribed: Model of ancient jug dredged from the sea off Great Yarmouth, now in the museum. Rd. No. 500870.

height 132mm. Price £40

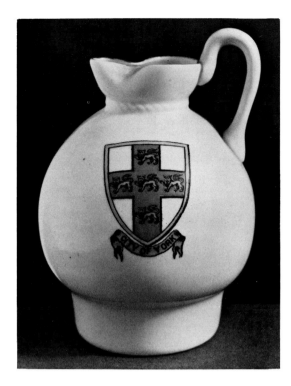

No. 306. York Ewer

Inscribed: York Ewer. From original in Hospitium. Found at York.

(a)	height	64mm.	Price	£3.50
(b)	height	132mm.	Price	£10

No. 307. York Urn

Inscribed: Roman urn, from original in Hospitium. Found at York.

(a)	height	50mm.	Price	£3.25
(b)	height	96mm.	Price	£8

No. 308. York Vessel

Inscribed: Roman vessel. From original in hospitium. Found at York.

height   73mm.   Price   £10

FIRST WORLD WAR

No. 309. British Shrapnel Shell
Inscribed: Model of British 6in incendiary shell.

height   110mm.   Price   £14

No. 310. British Tank

Inscribed: Model of British tank — "England expects that every tank will do its damn'dest. Copyright.

length   110mm.   Price   £29.50

No. 312. Maldon Incendiary Bomb

Inscribed: Model of incendiary bomb dropped at Maldon 16 April 1915 from a German zeppelin. Copyright.

height   75mm.   Price   £16.50

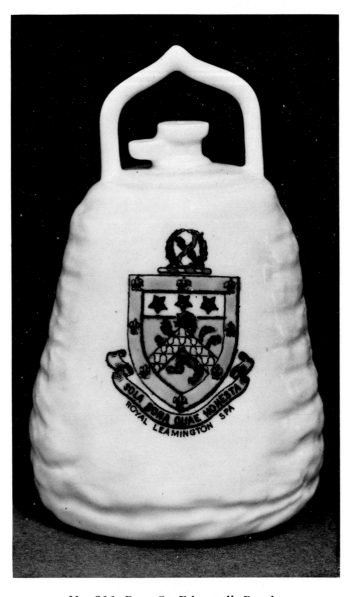

No. 311. Bury St. Edmund's Bomb

Inscribed: Model of German bomb dropped on Bury St. Edmunds from a Zeppelin 30 April 1915. Copyright.

height   75mm.   Price   £16.50

No. 313. Russian Shrapnel Shell

Inscribed: Model of Russian shrapnel shell. The original was captured by the Huns and fired by them at the British. Copyright.

height   110mm.   Price   £14.50

FOOTWARE

No. 314. Boulogne Wooden Shoe

Inscribed: Model of wooden shoes worn by the fisherwomen of Boulogne sur mer and Le Portal. Rd. No. 539421.

length 118mm. Price £18.50

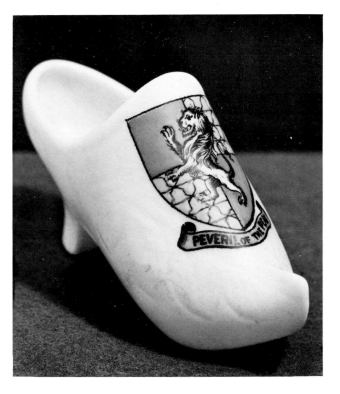

No. 315. Dinant Wooden Shoe

Inscribed: Model of wooden shoe worn at Dinant.

length 74mm. Price £14.50

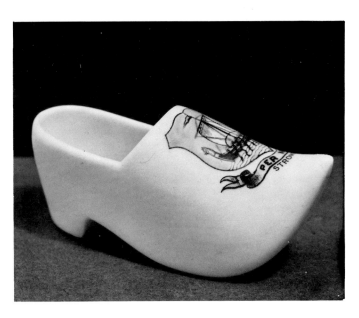

No. 316. Dutch Sabot

Inscribed: Model of Dutch Sabot.

length 82mm. Price £12

No. 317. Lancashire Clog

Inscribed: Model of Lancashire clog. Copyright.

length 93mm. Price £35

The correct Arms for this model is reputed to be Accrington. In the compiler's opinion any Lancashire 'Cotton' Town would be equally acceptable.

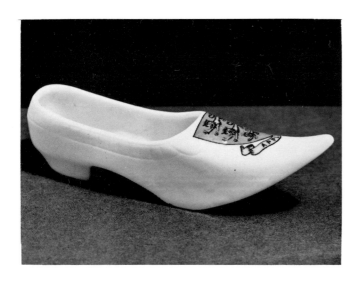

No. 318. Norwegian Wooden Shoe

Inscribed: Model of Norwegian Shoe.

length   103mm.   Price   £16

No. 319 Queen Elizabeth's Riding Shoe

Inscribed: Model of Queen Elizabeth's riding shoe formerly at Horham Hall, Thaxted.

length   105mm.   Price   £85

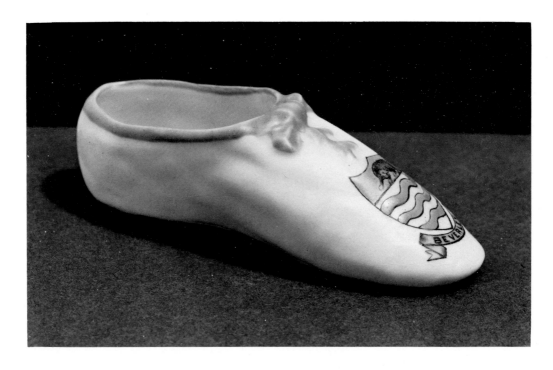

No. 320. Queen Victoria's First Shoe

Inscribed: Model, exact size, of first shoes worn by Princess Victoria — H.M. late Queen — (who died Jan. 22nd 1901) made at Sidmouth in 1819.

length   102mm.   Price   £17.50

Models often include a leaflet relating the story behind this particular piece and the price with this included would be £28.

The sole of the model is pale yellow with a brown border.

FONTS

No. 321. Buckland Monachorum Font

Inscribed: Model of ancient Saxon font about 1000 years old discovered in foundations of Buckland Monachorum church in 1857 after being buried 400 years now in St. Paul's Church, Yelverton. Copyright.

height   74mm.   Price   £250

No. 322. Calne Ancient Saxon Font

Inscribed: Model of ancient Saxon font in Avebury Church near Calne, Wilts. Rd. No. 617575.

(a)	White	height	85mm.	Price	£100
(b)	Brown	height	85mm.	Price	£275

No. 323. Haddon Hall Font

Inscribed: Model of Norman font found at Haddon Hall (as shown in illustration).

(a)	White	height	92mm.	Price	£50
(b)	Brown	height	92mm.	Price	£275

Inscription on brown piece is on the base.

No. 324. Hereford Cathedral Font

Inscribed: Model of font in Hereford Cathedral the figures of 12 Apostles were partly erased by the Puritans.

(a)	White	height	96mm.	Price	£120
(b)	Brown	height	96mm.	Price	£300

No. 325. St. Iltyd's Font, Llantwit Major

Reputed inscription: Model of Norman font in St. Iltyd's Church, Llantwit Major etc.

height   90mm.   Price   £1,000

No. 326. St. Ives Font

Inscribed: Model of ancient font in St. Ives Church, Cornwall.
Rd. No. 594379.

	White glazed	height	86mm.	Price	£22.50
(a)	White unglazed	height	86mm.	Price	£125
(b)	Brown	height	86mm.	Price	£200

No. 328. St. Tudno's Font

Inscribed: Model of ancient font in St. Tudno's Church
Llandudno. Rd. No. 546713.

height   92mm.   Price   £22.50

No. 327. St. Martin's Font

Inscribed: Model of font (restored) in which King Ethelbert
was baptised by St. Augustine in St. Martin's Church
Canterbury. (Order of wording in inscription varies in the
different models).

(a)	White glazed, open	height	69mm.	Price	£40
(b)	White glazed, lidded	height	72mm.	Price	£35
(c)	Brown, open	height	69mm.	Price	£200
(d)	Brown, lidded	height	72mm.	Price	£200
(e)	White unglazed, lidded	height	72mm.	Price	£100
(f)	White glazed, dished	height	72mm.	Price	£35

The lidded model has the lid fixed and it cannot be removed.

No. 329. Shakespeare's Font

Inscribed: Model of font in which Shakespeare was baptised.
(clearly visible in illustration)

height   50mm.   Price   £20

This piece was modelled damaged, showing the condition of
the original at the time.

No. 330. Southwell Cathedral Font

Inscribed: Model of Font in Southwell Cathedral.

(a)	White glazed	height	95mm.	Price	£125
(b)	White unglazed	height	95mm.	Price	£150
(c)	Brown	height	95mm.	Price	£225

No variety carries a Coat of Arms.

No. 331. Warwick, Troy House Font

Inscribed: Model of ancient font at Troy House, Monmouth.

(a)	White glazed	height	52mm.	Price	£40
(b)	White unglazed	height	52mm.	Price	£50
(c)	Brown	height	52mm.	Price	£200

No. 332. Winchester Cathedral Font

No inscription.

(a)	White unglazed	height	130mm.	Price	£550
(b)	Black	height	113mm.	Price	£750

LIGHTHOUSES

No. 333. Beachy Head Lighthouse
Inscribed: Model of Beachy Head Lighthouse. Rd. No. 622475.

(a)	Brown band	height	125mm.	Price	£32.50
(b)	Black band	height	125mm.	Price	£35

No. 334. Braunton Lighthouse
Inscribed: Model of Braunton Lighthouse near Westwood Ho. Copyright.

height   133mm.   Price   £275

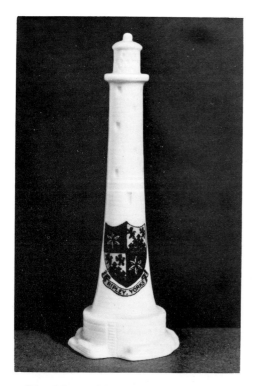

No. 336. Eddystone Lighthouse
Inscribed: Model of Eddystone Lighthouse.
height   125mm.   Price   £16.50

No. 335. Chicken Rock Lighthouse
Inscribed: Model of Chicken Rock Lighthouse, Isle of Man.
Rd. No. 602906.

height   127mm.   Price   £19.50

No. 335a. Dungeness Lighthouse
height   125mm.   Price   £150
Identical to Beachy Head Lighthouse.

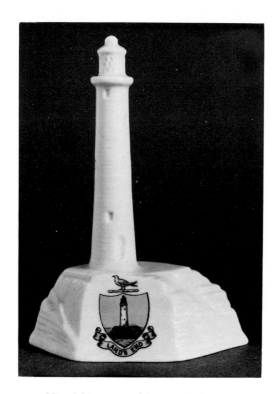

No. 337. Longships Lighthouse
Inscribed: Model of the Longships Lighthouse Land's End.
height   122mm.   Price   £22.50

No. 338. North Foreland Lighthouse

Inscribed: Model of the North Foreland Lighthouse. Rd. No. 639537.

height   108mm.   Price   £35

No. 340. St. Mary's Lighthouse

Inscribed: Model of St. Mary's Lighthouse, Whitley Bay. Copyright.

height   135mm.   Price   £300

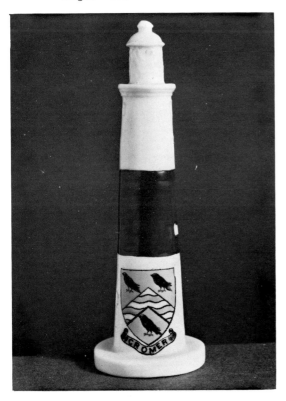

No. 339. Portland Lighthouse

Inscribed: Model of the Portland Lighthouse. Rd. No. 622476.

(a)	Brown band	height	120mm.	Price	£32.50
(b)	Black band	height	120mm.	Price	£60
(c)	Red band	height	120mm.	Price	£75

No. 341. Teignmouth Lighthouse

Inscribed: Model of Teignmouth Lighthouse. Rd. No. 622474.

height   115mm.   Price   £29.50

ANIMALS

Bear with Ragged Staff. No. 467. White glazed with the Warwick Coat of Arms on turquoise ground. Height 90mm. Also found in unglazed and coloured forms. Fairly rare.

No. 342. Aylesbury Duck

Inscribed: Model of the Aylesbury duck. Copyright.

length of base   100mm.   Price   £225

No. 343. Bear

No inscription.

        length   126mm.   Price   £300

'Polar bear' would appear to be a truer title for this piece.

No. 344. Bull

No inscription.

length of base   135mm.   Price   £350

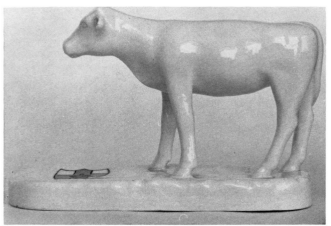

No. 345. Calf

No inscription.

length of base   117mm.   Price   £300

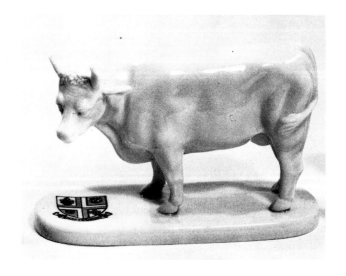

No. 347. Cow

No inscription.

Approximate length   90mm.   Price   £300

No. 346. Cheshire Cat

Inscribed around edge of base: "He grins like a Cheshire cat chewing gravel". Inscribed under base: Copyright.

length of base   83mm.   Price   £50

See appendix for Goss/England model.

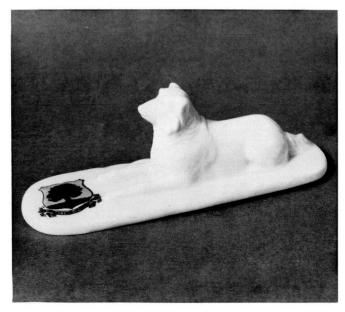

No. 348. Dog

No inscription.

length of base   133mm.   Price   £300

This model is identical in design to No. 354. Prince Llewellyn's dog.

No. 349. Hippopotamus

No inscription

length of base   127mm.   Price   £300

No. 349a. Kangaroo
Price   £500

No. 349b. Jaguar
Price   £600

No. 350. Lion

No inscription.

length of base   135mm.   Price   £300

No. 351. Lion (Wembley)

No inscription.

length of base   102mm.   Price   £125

The illustration gives an example of the Blackpool Arms that were so often used on 'seconds' by Mr. Naylor, the Blackpool agent. This reduces value to around £75.

No. 352. Lucerne Lion

Inscribed on base: The Lion of Lucerne. Rd. No. 589059. Inscribed on front as illustrated. Inscribed on back: four lines in Latin.

(a)	White	length	110mm.	Price	£75
(b)	Brown	length	110mm.	Price	£300.

Often found without the Latin wording and carrying the Blackpool Arms. These would be 'seconds' and worth £20.

No. 353. Penguin

Inscribed: Made in England. (Often missing).

length of base   83mm.   Price   £300

Correct Coats of Arms for this piece is 'Falkland Islands'. (Illustration by courtesy of City Museum and Art Gallery, Stoke-on-Trent.)

No. 355. Racehorse

Inscribed: Model of racehorse (not on all models).

length of base   120mm.   Price   £300

No. 354. Prince Llewellyn's Dog

Inscribed on top of base: Prince Llewellyn's dog "Gelert".

length of base   133mm.   Price   £500

Identical in design to No. 348. Dog.

No. 356. Rhinoceros

No inscription.

approximate length   135mm.   Price   £300

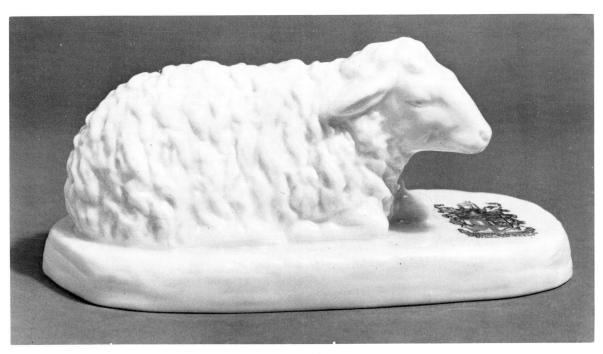

No. 357. Sheep

No inscription.

length of base   147mm.   Price   £250

No. 358. Shetland Pony

No inscription.

length of base   103mm.   Price   £175

See appendix for Goss/England model.

CROSSES

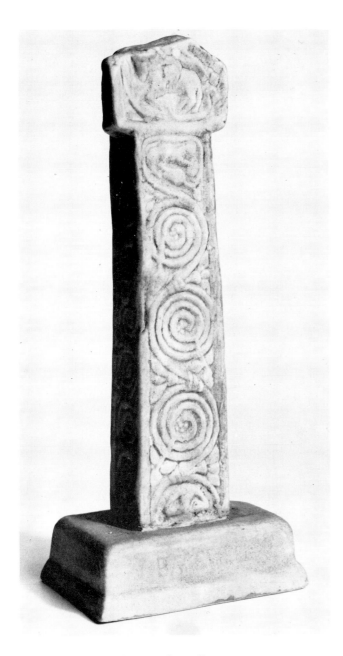

No. 360. Banbury Cross

Inscribed front: Banbury Cross.
Inscribed left front: Ride a cock horse to Banbury Cross.
Inscribed right front: To see a fine lady ride on a white horse.

   (a)   Glazed white   height   145mm.   Price £120
   (b)   Brown   height   145mm.   Price £180

The white model bears arms on the flat surface at bottom front. Usually marked GOSS/ENGLAND.

No. 360c. Old Market Cross, Buxton

   grey   height   88mm.   Price   £1,200

No. 359. Bakewell Cross

Impressed bottom front: Bakewell.

   (a)   White   height   150mm.   Price   £200
   (b)   Brown   height   150mm.   Price   £250

No. 361. Campbeltown Cross

Inscribed: Model of the Campbeltown Cross.

   height   145mm.   Price   £500

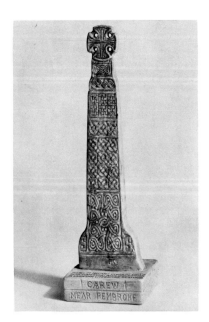

No. 362. Carew Cross

Impressed bottom front: Carew near Pembroke. Inscribed on front step: Model of ancient cross at Carew near Pembroke with inscription in unknown literature restored.

(a)	Brown	height	150mm.	Price	£150
(b)	Brown	height	216mm.	Price	£300
(c)	White unglazed	height	150mm.	Price	£150
(d)	White glazed	height	216mm.	Price	£200

No. 363. Eyam Cross

Impressed bottom front: Eyam

(a)	White glazed	height	170mm.	Price	£150
(b)	White unglazed	height	170mm.	Price	£200
(c)	Brown	height	170mm.	Price	£300

No. 364. Inverary Cross of the Nobles

Impressed bottom front: Inverary cross. Inscribed on back: This is the cross of the Nobles, viz:— Duncan, Mcomyn, Patrick his son and Ludovick the son of Patrick who caused the cross to be erected.

height   145mm.   Price   £600

Only known coloured brown.

No. 365. Kirk Bradden Cross

Inscribed on back: Model of cross at Kirk Bradden I. of Man probably more than 1000 years old.

height   84mm.   Price   £65

No. 366. Llandaff Cross

Impressed on front: Llandaff.

height 150mm. Price £450

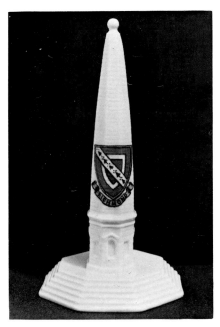

No. 367. Richmond Market Cross

Inscribed: Model of the cross in the Market Place, Richmond, Yorkshire. Rebuilt 1771.

(a)	White	height	130mm.	Price	£30
(b)	Brown	height	130mm.	Price	£300

No. 368. St. Buryan Cross

Inscribed: Model of ancient cross in St. Buryan Churchyard near Lands-End Cornwall.

(a)	White glazed	height	43mm.	Price	£75
(b)	White unglazed	height	43mm.	Price	£100
(c)	Brown	height	43mm.	Price	£150

No. 369. St. Column Major Cross

Impressed on back: Model of ancient cross in St. Columb Major Churchyard.

(a)	White glazed	height	90mm.	Price	£75
(b)	White unglazed	height	90mm.	Price	£75
(c)	Brown	height	90mm.	Price	£125

Also known without inscription, with Blackpool Arms (white unglazed — Price £50).

135

No. 370 St. Ives Cross

Impressed, bottom front: St. Ives Cornwall.

(a)	White	height	135mm.	Price	£200
(b)	White	height	202mm.	Price	£225
(c)	Brown	height	135mm.	Price	£300
(d)	Brown	height	202mm.	Price	£300

No. 371. St. Martin's Cross, Iona

Impressed, bottom front: St. Martin Iona.

(a)	Brown	height	145mm.	Price	£250
(b)	Brown	height	212mm.	Price	£300

Also in white glazed or unglazed — £200.

No. 372. Sandbach Crosses

Impressed, bottom front: Sanbach.

height 255mm.   Price   £1,250

One of the most illusive, impressive and sought after Goss models.

STATUES
and
MONUMENTS

No. 373. Barnet Stone

Inscribed front: (as shown in illustration). Back: From St. Albans VIII miles ¾. Left side: To Hatfield VII miles ¾. Right side: This was erected 1740.

(a)	White	height	167mm.	Price	£125
(b)	Brown	height	167mm.	Price	£250

No. 374. Cenotaph, Whitehall

Inscribed: The Cenotaph Whitehall.

(a)	White glazed	height	143mm.	Price	£32.50
(b)	White unglazed	height	143mm.	Price	£52.50

Smaller models are 'GOSS ENGLAND', see appendix.

No. 375. Cumbrae Monument

Impressed on front: The Monument Towmonted Cumbrae.

height 180mm. Price £350

This model is only known in brown.

No. 376. Edith Cavell Monument

Inscribed, left side: Humanity.
Inscribed, right side: Sacrifice.
Inscribed, back: Edith Cavell Nurse, patriot and martyr.

height   174mm.   Price   £52.50

No. 377. Fourshire Stone

Impressed on front: The Fourshire stone, Worcestershire. Impressed on left side: Gloucestershire. Impressed on right side: Oxfordshire. Impressed on back: Warwickshire. Inscribed on back: Model of the Fourshire Stone near Chipping Norton.

This stone marks the spot where the counties of Gloucester, Oxford, Warwick and Worcester meet.

height   118mm.   Price   £45

No. 378. Hambledon Cricket Stone

Inscribed on front: This stone marks the site of the ground of the Hambledon Cricket Club circ. 1760-1787.

height   80mm.   Price   £1,000

This model is only known in brown.

No. 379. King Alfred's Statue

details of size not available   Price   £75

This model is a late one and it is believed to occur with the 'W.H. GOSS ENGLAND' mark only. It is included in this section as the veracity of this is still in doubt.

No. 380. London Stone

Inscribed on front as illustrated. A lengthy inscription is found on each of the other three sides.

(a)	White unglazed	height	109mm.	Price	£125
(b)	Brown	height	109mm.	Price	£200

No. 381. Rothesey Stone

No inscription.

height   95mm.   Price   £450

This model is only known in brown. It is only 6mm. thick.

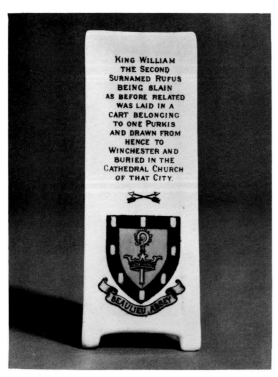

No. 382. Rufus Stone

Inscribed on front, as illustrated. Lengthy inscriptions are to be found on each of the other two sides, the model being triangular.

height   94mm.   Price   £8

No. 383. Sailor's Stone, Hindhead

This model is a late one and carries the "W.H. Goss England" mark.

height   95mm.   width   80mm.   Price   £55

The inscription is as illustrated below, (this was the only piece not illustrated in the first printing, and we are indebted to Mrs. L.E. Howard of California for the photographs).

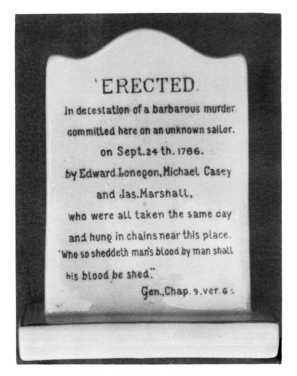

No. 383. Inscription

details of size not available   Price   £55

No. 384. St. Cuthbert's Statue

Inscribed on front: St. Cuthbert Durham.

height   133mm.   Price   £400

MODELS issued to MEMBERS of the LEAGUE of GOSS COLLECTORS and the INTERNATIONAL LEAGUE of GOSS COLLECTORS

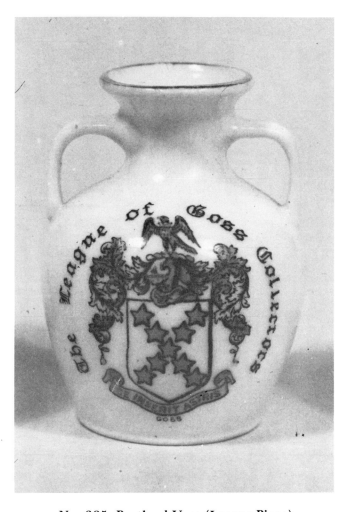

No. 386. Ancient Costril (League Piece)

Inscribed on front as illustrated. Inscribed on base: Model of ancient costril or pilgrims' bottle. Rd. No. 526382.

This model is only issued to members of the League, and cannot be bought.

    (a)   height   55mm.   Price   £40
    (b)   height   55mm.   Price   £55

(a) carries the 'League' Arms, as illustrated. (b) carries the 'International League' Arms as shown on models numbered 389 to 403.

No. 385. Portland Vase (League Piece)

Inscribed on front as shown in illustration. Inscribed on base: Model of the Portland Vase, in the British Museum.

        height   51mm.   Price   £25

Identical in design to No. 231.

No. 388. Anglo-Saxon Cinerary Urn (League Piece)

Inscribed on front as illustration. Inscribed on base: Model of Anglo-Saxon cinerary urn, found at King's Newton copyright.

This is only issued to members of more than 6 years standing and cannot be purchased.

(a)	height	60mm.	Price	£30
(b)	height	60mm.	Price	£40

(a) carries the 'League' Arms as illustrated. (b) carries the 'International League' Arms, as shown on models 389 to 403.

No. 387. Staffordshire Tyg (League Piece)

Inscribed on front as illustration. Inscribed on base: Model of ancient Staffordshire tyg. Rd. No. 641312.

This model is only issued to members of more than 4 years standing and cannot be purchased.

(a)	height	70mm.	Price	£40
(b)	height	70mm.	Price	£50

(a) carries the 'League' Arms as illustrated. (b) carries the 'International League' Arms, as shown on models 389 to 403.

No. 389. Cirencester Roman Ewer (League Piece)

Inscribed on front as illustrated. 1(b).
Inscribed on base: Model of Roman ewer found at Cirencester Issued to members only and cannot be purchased. Copyright.

(a)	height	78mm.	Price	£40
(b)	height	78mm.	Price	£65

(a) carries the 'League' Arms as shown on models numbered 385 to 388.
(b) carries the 'International League' Arms as illustration.

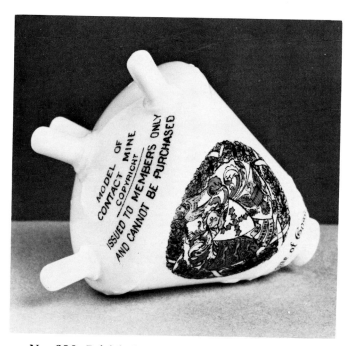

No. 390. British Contact Mine (League Piece)

Inscribed below the Arms: International League of Goss Collectors.
Inscribed on large end: Model of contact mine.
Copyright. Issued to members only and cannot be purchased.

length   73mm.   Price   £90

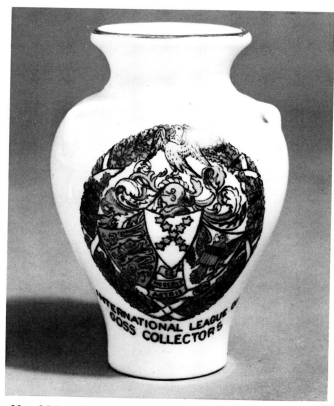

No. 391. Ashmolean Vase, Gnossus (League Piece)

Inscribed on front as illustrated.
Inscribed on base: Model of ancient vase from Gnossus No.
110 in Ashmolean Museum.
Issued to members only and cannot be purchased. Copyright.

height   60mm.   Price   £50

No. 392. Greek Amphora Vase (League Piece)

Inscribed on front, as illustrated.
Inscribed on base: Model of Greek Amphora vase (circa
350 B.C.) which was given filled with oil as a prize in the
Panathenaic Games.
This model is only issued to members of the league and
cannot be bought.

height   138mm.   Price   £50

No. 393. Italian Krater (League Piece)

Inscribed on front as illustrated.
Inscribed on base: Model of Italian Krater from the original
in the British Museum. This model is only issued to members
of the league and cannot be bought.

height   100mm.   Price   £70

No. 394. Egyptian Lotus Vase (League Piece)

Inscribed on front as illustrated.
Inscribed on base: Model of ancient Egyptian lotus vase.
Copyright. Issued to members only & cannot be purchased.
1923.

height   80mm.   Price   £150

No. 395. Tetinae or Feeding Bottle (League Piece)

Inscribed on front as illustrated.
Inscribed on base: Model of Roman tetinae or feeding bottle
found at Wilderspool — Copyright 1924.
This model is only issued to members of the League and can-
not be bought.

height   105mm.   Price   £80

In the photograph the spout is just visible on reverse of model.

No. 396. Mycenaean Vase, Cyprus (League Piece)

Inscribed on front as illustrated.
Inscribed on base: Model of Mycenaean vase from Cyprus in
British Museum. Copyright 1925.
This model is only issued to members of the League and can-
not be bought.

diameter of rim   90mm.   Price   £75

No. 397. Staffordshire Drinking Cup (League Piece)

Inscribed on front as illustrated.
Inscribed on base: Model of Staffordshire drinking cup
circa 1650. Copyright.
This model is only issued to members of the league and
cannot be bought.

height   111mm.   Price   £70

This model carries a handle, not visible in illustration.

No. 398. Colchester Roman Lamp (League Piece)

Inscribed on front as illustrated.
Inscribed on base: Model of Roman lamp found at Colchester.
Copyright 1927.
This model is only issued to members of the league and cannot be bought.

length   100mm.   Price   £175

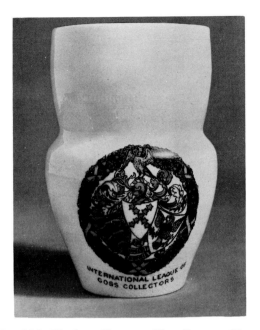

No. 399. Fimber Cinerary Urn (League Piece)

Inscribed on front as illustrated.
Inscribed on base: Model of ancient British cinerary urn found at Fimber. Copyright 1928.
This model is only issued to members of the league and cannot be bought.

height   106mm.   Price   £150

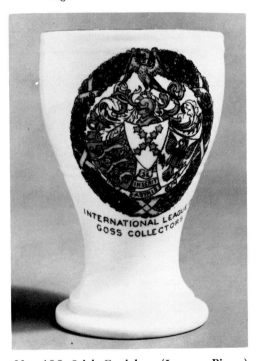

No. 400. Irish Cruisken (League Piece)

Inscribed on front as illustrated.
Inscribed on base: Model of ancient Irish cruisken. Copyright 1929.
This model is issued to members of the league and cannot be bought.

height   95mm.   Price   £150

No. 401. Northwich Sepulchral Urn (League Piece)

Inscribed on front as illustrated.
Inscribed on base: Model of Britano-Roman sepulchral urn found near Northwich (Salinae) now in Warrington Museum. Copyright 1930.
This model is only issued to members of the league and cannot be purchased.

height   85mm.   Price   £225

No. 403. Chester Roman Urn. (League piece)

*Inscribed: Model of Roman Urn found at Condate (Kinderton)
Cheshire 1820, copyright 1932. This model is only issued to
members of the league and cannot be bought.*

height   90mm.   Price   £200

No. 402. Chester Roman Altar (League Piece)

Inscription on front as illustrated.
*Inscription on reverse: "This model is only issued to members
of the league and cannot be bought". "Copyright 1931".*

*The crest is also shown on back with normal inscription
below.*

height   117mm.   Price   £350

BUILDINGS
(uncoloured)

No. 405. Blackgang Tower

Inscribed: Model of Tower on St. Catherine's Hill, Blackgang, I.W. Built in 1323 by W. De Godyton for a chantry priest to sing mass for the souls of mariners and in the tower a light was placed to warn ships off this dangerous coast. Rd. No. 630366.

height   112mm.   Price   £20

No. 406. Blackpool Tower

Inscribed: Model of Blackpool Tower.

height   118mm.   Price   £32.50

The arms are on back of model.

Examples of buildings with the following numbers are known in uncoloured and coloured models. Please refer to Alphabetical list of Contents for numbers 404, 407, 412, 414, 415 and 418.

No. 408. Grinlow Tower

Reputed inscription: Model of Grinlow Tower (known as Soleman's Temple). The building was erected by public subscription and stands on the site of a prehistoric barrow explored in 1894. Copyright.

height 95mm. Price £200

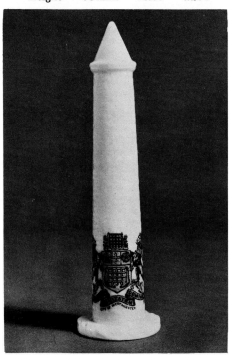

No. 410. Largs Tower

Inscribed: Model of Battle of Largs Memorial Tower. Rd. No. 610012.

height 128mm. Price £30

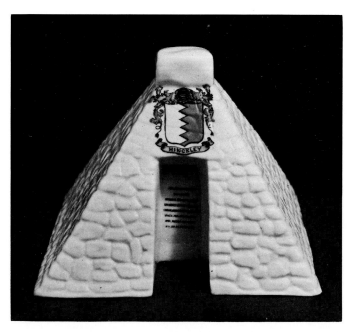

No. 409. King Richard's Well Cover

Inscribed: Model of structure covering King Richard's well on Bosworth field. Copyright.

Translation of inscription: With water drawn from this well Richard III, King of England, assuaged his thirst (when) fighting in the most desperate and hostile manner with Henry, Earl of Richmond, and about to lose before night his life, together with his sceptre. August 22. (O.S.) A.D. 1485.

length of base 100mm. Price £175

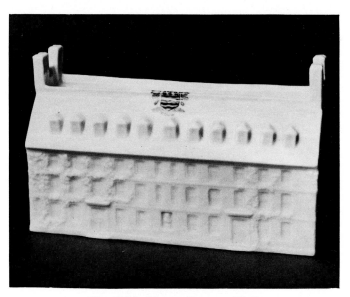

No. 411. Massachusetts Hall

Inscribed: Massachsetts Hall 1718–1720, Harvard University Cambridge, Mass. Rd. No. 647235 Jones McBuffee and Stratton Co., 33, Franklyn St. Boston Mass.

length 170mm. Price £1,000

This piece is only known white, with Blackpool Arms, but it is probable that it also exists coloured.

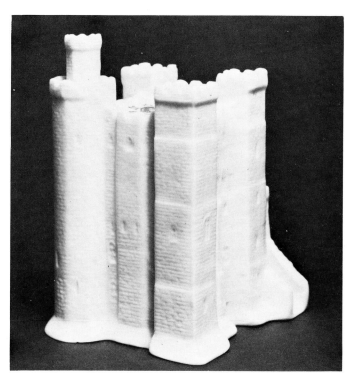

No. 413. Newcastle Keep

Inscribed: The Castle — Newcastle on Tyne. Robert Curthose eldest son of the Conqueror, built a fortress here in 1080, which, in contradistinction to the old Roman castrum of Pons Aelii, was called the new castle, whence the present name of the town. Copyright.

	White	height	88mm.	Price	£150
(a)	Brown	height	88mm.	Price	£350

No. 417. Skegness Clock Tower

Inscribed: Model of the Clock Tower Skegness.

height   132mm.   Price   £100

No. 416. Sir John Barrow's Tower

Inscribed: Model of Sir John Barrow's monument Ulverston. Copyright. "In honour of Sir John Barrow Bart. Erected A.D. 1850".

height   120mm.   Price   £75

No. 419. Windleshaw Chantry

Inscribed: A present from Lowe House new church bazaar 1920 model of Windleshaw Chantry, in St. Helens Catholic burial ground. Founded by Sir Thomas Gerard of Bryn, after the Battle of Agincourt (A.D. 1415), for a priest to celebrate mass there for the souls of his ancestors for ever. The last priest was Richard Frodsham, of Wyndle (A.D. 1548).

height   128mm.   Price   £75

The Arms are the same on all models. This was one of the rarest models until some twenty came to light in the early 1970s.

BUILDINGS
(coloured)

No. 420. Abbot's Kitchen, Glastonbury

Inscribed: Model of abbot's kitchen Glastonbury Abbey. Copyright.

height   88mm.   Price   £550

There are two varieties, one pale brown with black doors, the other, pale brown with green mossy markings and red doors. Both same value.

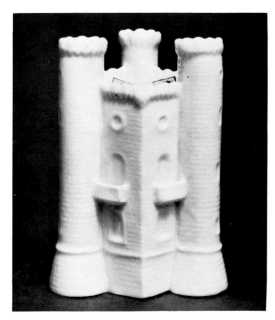

No. 422. Broadway Tower

Inscribed: Model of Broadway tower. Rd. No. 634630.

(a)	White	height	75mm.	Price	£110
(b)	Grey	height	75mm.	Price	£200
(c)	Brown	height	75mm.	Price	£300

The white model usually carries arms on the top in the hollow between the towers.

No. 421. Bargate, Southampton

Inscribed: The Bargate Southampton. Of the seven gates which formerley gave entrance to Southampton only two now remain. Of these the finest is the bargate which contains Norman work. etc. etc. etc. Rd. No. 594375.

(a)	White glazed	height	55mm.	Price	£65
(b)	White glazed	height	87mm.	Price	£85
(c)	Grey	height	87mm.	Price	£140
(d)	Brown	height	87mm.	Price	£200

The glazed models do not carry arms.

No. 423. Bunyan's Cottage, Elstow

Inscribed: John Bunyan's cottage, Elstow, Bedfordshire. John Bunyan was born in this parish in 1628, not far from this spot and lived in this cottage after his marriage in 1649. Copyright.

length   60mm.   Price   £850

No. 424. Burns's Cottage

Inscribed: Model of Burns' cottage Robert Burns the Ayrshire poet was born on the 25th. January A.D. 1759 died 21st. July A.D. 1796 aged 37½ years. Rd. No. 211037.

(a)	Glazed	length	62mm.	Price	£55
(b)	Unglazed	length	62mm.	Price	£55
(c)	Glazed	length	145mm.	Price	£100
(d)	Unglazed	length	145mm.	Price	£100

The large size is in the form of a night light.

No. 425. Cat and Fiddle Inn, Buxton

Inscribed: Model of the Cat-Fiddle-Inn Nr. Buxton, 1690 feet above high sea level, the highest licensed house in England. Copyright.

length   65mm.   Price   £185

No. 426. Charles Dickens's House, Gadshill

Inscribed: Model of Charles Dickens' House Gad's Hill, Rochester. Rd. No. 630367.

(a)	Dark brown	length	65mm.	Price	£90
(b)	Brick-red	length	65mm.	Price	£90

An interesting variety can be found with the two small windows at the side of the door missing — same price.

No. 427. Dove Cottage, Grasmere

Inscribed: Model of Dove Cottage, Grasmere. The home of Wordsworth 1799 to 1808. Now the Wordsworth Memorial. Copyright.

length   102mm.   Price   £375

No. 428. Feathers Hotel, Ledbury

Inscribed: Model of Feathers Hotel, Ledbury. Copyright.

length   114mm.   Price   £650

No. 429. First and Last House

Inscribed: First and last house in England. Rd. No. 521645. (some models state 'Standing on the extreme point of Land's End')

1(a)	Grey roof glazed	length	64mm.	Price	£60
(b)	Grey roof unglazed	length	64mm.	Price	£60
(c)	Cream roof glazed	length	64mm.	Price	£55
(d)	Cream roof unglazed	length	64mm.	Price	£55
(e)	Night light	length	117mm.	Price	£200
2	With annex	length	150mm.	Price	£550

No. 2 is the same as 1(a) in design with an extension with another chimney at the end and additional six-paned window with shutters.

No. 430. First and Last Post Office

Inscribed: Model of the first and last post office in England at Sennen, Cornwall. Rd. No. 618950.

length   73mm.   Price   £135

No. 431. Goss Oven

Inscribed: Model of oven in which Goss porcelain is fired. Copyright.

(a)	Glossy dark brown	length	75mm.	Price	£175
(b)	Matt brick-red	length	75mm.	Price	£150

No. 432. Gretna Green, The Old Toll Bar

Inscribed in script. Old Toll Bar, Gretna Green, over 10,000 marriages performed in the marriage room. est. 1830. Copyright.

length   125mm.   Price   £1,500

No. 433. Gullane Smithy

Inscribed: Model of old smithy, Gullane, N.B. Copyright.

length   75mm.   Price   £550

No. 434. Ann Hathaway's Cottage

Inscribed: Model of Ann Hathaway's Cottage Shottery near Stratford-on-Avon. Rd. No. 208047.

(a)	Glazed	length	62mm.	Price	£50
(b)	Unglazed	length	62mm.	Price	£50
(c)	Glazed	length	148mm.	Price	£125
(d)	Unglazed	length	148mm.	Price	£125

The large size is in the form of a night light.

Three sizes exist in a cruder form, often referred to as "Willow Art Mould". These are very late models and would seem to qualify for the "GOSS/ENGLAND" Mark.

No. 435. Thomas Hardy's House

Inscribed: Model of the birthplace of Thomas Hardy the Wessex poet Dorchester. Copyright.

length   100mm.   Price   £325

No. 436. Holden Chapel

Inscribed: Model of Holden Chapel, built 1744, Harvard University, Cambridge, Mass. Rd. No. 643867.

length 127mm. Price £1,500

This model is in the form of a night light.

No. 437. Hop Kiln, Headcorn

Inscribed: Hop Kiln, Head Corn, Kent.

height 89mm. Price £1,200

No. 438. Huer's House, Newquay

Inscribed: Model of Huer's House Newquay Cornwall. Rd. No. 610011.

(a)	Glazed	length	70mm.	Price	£85
(b)	Unglazed	length	70mm.	Price	£85

No. 439. Samuel Johnson's House, Lichfield

Inscribed: Model of the house in Lichfield in which Dr. Samuel Johnson was born. Born 1709 died 1784. Educated at Lichfield Grammar School buried in Westminster Abbey. Rd. No. 605733.

(a)	Glazed	height	75mm.	Price	£100
(b)	Unglazed	height	75mm.	Price	£100

No. 440. Joseph of Arimathea's Church

Inscribed: Model of church built by Joseph of Arimathea A.D.
63 at Glastonbury. The first christian church in England. Built
of willows and thatched with rushes, it stood on the site now
occupied by St. Joseph's chapel, Glastonbury Abbey. From a
drawing in the British Museum.

length   70mm.   Price   £650

No. 441. John Knox's House

Inscribed: Model of the house in Edinburgh where John Knox
the Scottish reformer died 24th. Nov. 1572.

height   100mm.   Price   £250

This piece was the latest new model of a coloured building
made and carries the word "ENGLAND" below the normal
Goss Mark.

No. 442. Ledbury Market

Inscribed: Model of ye old market house, Ledbury. Copyright.

length   68mm.   Price   £250

No. 443. Prince Llewelyn's House, Beddgelert

Inscribed: Model of Prince Llewelyn's house Beddgelert. Rd.
No. 594374.

(a)	Glazed	length	63mm.	Price	£85
(b)	Unglazed	length	63mm.	Price	£85

No. 444. Lloyd George's House

Inscribed: Rt. Hon. D. Lloyd George's early home Llanystymdwy, Criccieth. Rd. No. 617573.

1(a)	Glazed	length	62mm.	Price	£120
(b)	Unglazed	length	62mm.	Price	£120
2	With annex length		101mm.	Price	£90

No. 446. Manx Cottage, Laxey

Inscribed: Model of Manx Cottage. Rd. No. 273243.

(a)	Glazed	length	62mm.	Price	£70
(b)	Unglazed	length	62mm.	Price	£70
(c)	Glazed	length	122mm.	Price	£125
(d)	Unglazed	length	122mm.	Price	£125

The large size is in the form of a night light.

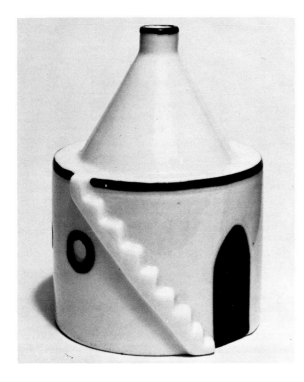

No. 445. Look Out House, Newquay

Inscribed: Model of look out house Newquay, Cornwall. Rd. No. 605735.

(a)	Four portholes	height	65mm.	Price	£75
(b)	Five portholes	height	65mm.	Price	£75

No. 447. Monnow Gate

Inscribed: Model of Monnow Gate Monmouth.

(a)	White glazed	height	95mm.	Price	£80
(b)	Brown	height	95mm.	Price	£250

The white model carries Coats of Arms on each end.

No. 448. Norman Tower, Christchurch

Inscribed: Model of Norman tower, Priory Church Christchurch, circa 1100, built by Ralph Flambard Bishop of Durham 1099-1128. Rd. No. 567379.

(a)	White unglazed	height 123mm.	Price	£80
(b)	Grey	height 123mm.	Price	£100
(c)	Brown	height 123mm.	Price	£300

No. 449. Old Court House, Christchurch

Inscribed: Model of the Old Court House built 1511 Castle Street Christchurch, Hants. Copyright.

length　　76mm.　　Price　　£245

An L-shaped building. The size given is for front of model.

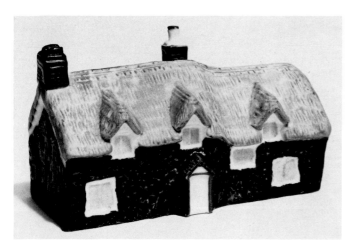

No. 450. Old Maid's Cottage, Lee

Inscription: Model of old maid's cottage at Lee, Devon. Rd. No. 622406.

(a)	Glazed	length 73mm.	Price	£85
(b)	Unglazed	length 73mm.	Price	£85

No. 451. Old Thatched Cottage, Poole

Inscribed: Model of the old thatched cottage Poole. Copyright.

length　　68mm.　　Price　　£375

No. 452. Portman Lodge, Bournemouth

Inscribed: Portman Lodge the second house built in Bournemouth. Copyright. Built by Squire Tregonwell about 1810 & called "Tregonwell House" name altered to "Portman Lodge" when it was occupied by Lord Portman.

    see below for size Price £325

An L-shaped building 84mm. on long side and 72mm. on shorter side (with door).

An interesting variety can be found with a partly closed door, whilst on others only an aperture is found.

No. 453. Priest's House, Prestbury

Inscribed: 786 model of priests house Prestbury, Cheshire. Copyright.

  height to top of chimney 71mm. Price £1,000

No. 454. Reculver Towers

Inscribed: Model of Reculver Towers. Rd. No. 639536.

(a)	Glazed white	height	101mm.	Price	£90
(b)	Grey	height	101mm.	Price	£225
(c)	Brown	height	101mm.	Price	£250

(a) has Coats of Arms on the side of each tower.

No. 455. St. Catherine's Abbotsbury

Inscribed: Model of St. Catherine's Chapel, Abbotsbury, Dorset. Copyright.

  length 87mm. Price £400

No. 456. St. Nicholas Chapel, Ilfracombe

Inscribed on gable end: Model of St. Nicholas Chapel, Lantern Hill, Ilfracombe. Which up to the time of Henry VIII was used as a place of worship for sailors. Rd. No. 613770

(a)	Glazed	length	74mm.	Price	£100
(b)	Unglazed	length	74mm.	Price	£100

No. 457. St. Nicholas Chapel, St. Ives

Inscribed on gable end: Model of the ancient Chapel of St. Nicholas, St. Ives, Cornwall partially destroyed by order of the War Office, 1904 rebuilt and restored by Sir Edward Hain 1911. Rd. No. 602905.

length 55mm. Price £200

This model is also known uncoloured, in which state it could possibly be a "second".

No. 458. Shakespeare's House

Inscribed: Model of Shakespeare's House. Rd. No. 225833.

1	(a)	Full length as illustrated	Glazed	length	78mm.	Price	£50
	(b)	Full length as illustrated	Unglazed	length	78mm.	Price	£50
	(c)	Full length as illustrated	Glazed	length	186mm.	Price	£135
	(d)	Full length as illustrated	Unglazed	length	186mm.	Price	£135
2		Half length	length	71mm.	height	80mm.	Price	£65
3		Half length with loose base	length of base		109mm.	Price	£85

1(c), 1(d) and 3 are in the form of night lights. A smaller version of No. 1 has been seen, length 64mm., but it is very poor as the front has sunk during firing. It is not thought that this size was in general production. Four sizes of the full length model are also known in a cruder design, often referred to as "Willow Art Mould" and it would appear that they qualify for the "GOSS/ENGLAND" section.

No. 459. Sulgrave Manor

Inscribed: Model of Sulgrave Manor Co. Northampton, England.
Rd. No. 638372. Lawrence Washington had a grant of Sulgrave
30 Hen. VIII. His great-grandson John Washington went to
America about 1657 and was the great-grandfather of George
Washington.

Overall length 125mm.   Price   £1,000

No. 460. Tenby Gate

Inscribed: Model of south west gateway (known as five
arches) in the town walls of Tenby. The walls date from
the reign of Edward III about 1328. Copyright.

(a)	Glazed white	height 65mm.	Price	£100
(b)	Coloured	height 65mm.	Price	£250

No. 461. "A Window in Thrums"

Inscribed: "A window in Thrums". Rd. No. 322142.

(a)	Glazed	length	60mm.	Price	£85
(b)	Unglazed	length	60mm.	Price	£85
(c)	Unglazed	length	130mm.	Price	£200

The large size is in the form of a night-light.

No. 462. Ellen Terry's Farm

Inscribed: Model of Miss Ellen Terry's Farm near Tenterden,
Kent. Rd. No. 641313.

(a)	Glossy dark brown roof	length	70mm.	Price £325
(b)	Brick-red roof	length	70mm.	Price £325

No. 463. Tudor House, Southampton

Inscribed: Tudor House, Southampton, built 1535. Also a long inscription on back regarding its Royal visitors.

Overall length   83mm.   Price   £245

No. 464. Isaac Walton's Cottage

Inscribed: Model of Isaac Walton's Birthplace, Shallowford.

(a)	length	82mm.	Price	£725
(b)	length	88mm.	Price	£725

The large size also carries the number '834' and despite the slight difference in length looks considerably larger.

No. 465. Wordsworth's House

Inscribed: Model of Wordswoth's birthplace Cockermouth. Rd. No. 639535.

length   81mm.   Price   £185

UNCLASSIFIED

No. 467. Bear with Ragged Staff

No inscription.

(a)	White glazed	height	90mm.	Price	£75
(b)	White unglazed	height	90mm.	Price	£100
(c)	Coloured	height	90mm.	Price	£200

Only (a) carries coats of arms.

No. 466. Acanthus Rose Bowl

Inscribed: The Acanthus rose bowl. Rd. No. 633431.

height   134mm.   Price   £75

To be complete this model should have a wire cover, not shown on our photograph.

Any Coat of Arms would be appropriate.

No. 468. Colchester Oyster Shell

No inscription.

length   68mm.   Price   £5

No. 470. Fisherwoman's Basket

No inscription.

(a)	length	80mm.	Price	£5.50
(b)	length	80mm.	Price	£7.50

No. 469. Devil over Lincoln

Impressed on sides of base: The Devil looking over Lincoln.

(a)	White	height	147mm.	Price	£50
(b)	Brown	height	147mm.	Price	£75

No. 471. Guillemot's Egg

No inscription.

length   83mm.   Price   £50

This model is found in different colours with the ground usually of brown or brey.

No. 472. Leek

Inscribed on back: K. Henry V. "The Welshmen did goot servace (at Crecy) in a garden where leeks did grow". Shakespeare.

height   90mm.   Price   £7.50

The leaf tips are coloured green for about 30mm.

No. 473. Limpet Shell

No inscription.

diameter   74mm.   Price   £5

This model stands on three attractive coral feet.

No. 474. Lincoln Imp

Impressed: The Imp of Lincoln.

(a) On pedestal as illustration
    height   112mm.   Price   £75
(b) Without pedestal
    White   height   75mm.   Price   £25
(c) White   height   107mm.   Price   £30
(d) White   height   145mm.   Price   £45
(e) Brown   height   75mm.   Price   £30
(f) Brown   height   107mm.   Price   £40
(g) Brown   height   145mm.   Price   £50

Can also be found 'outpressed' on mugs and tumblers.

No. 475. Loving Cup (Three-handled)

No inscription.

(a)	height	36mm.	Price	£4.50
(b)	height	42mm.	Price	£5.50
(c)	height	50mm.	Price	£6.50
(d)	height	60mm.	Price	£7.50
(e)	height	69mm.	Price	£8.50
(f)	height	80mm.	Price	£9.50
(g)	height	120mm.	Price	£35
(h)	height	135mm.	Price	£45

Some of the smaller sizes are to be found with square handles value 50% more than round handled models.

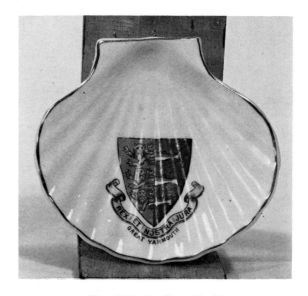

No. 476. Nautilus Shell

No inscription.

> height   152mm.   Price   £65

Mounted on attractive coral-coloured "legs".

No. 477. Old Horse Shoe

Inscribed as shown in illustration.

> height   115mm.   Price   £7.50

The dark colour in illustration is a display stand and not part of the model.

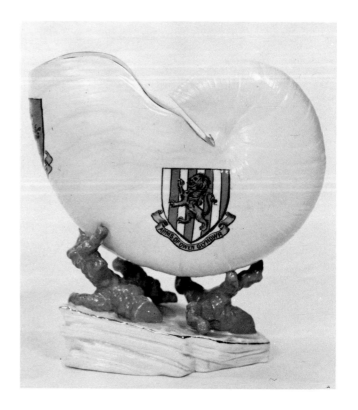

No. 478. Scallop Shell

No inscription.

(a)	length	76mm.	Price	£4.50
(b)	length	105mm.	Price	£7.50
(c)	length	125mm.	Price	£12

The model in the illustration is displayed on a stand.

No. 479. Stratford Toby Jug and Basin

Jug inscribed: Model of the Stratford Toby Jug. Basin not inscribed.

(a)	Jug	height	78mm.	Price	£45
(b)	Basin	height	53mm.	Price	£75

These two pieces are considered by most collectors as a "pair".

No. 480. Trusty Servant

Inscribed on base: A piece of antiquity painted on the wall adjoining the kitchen of Winchester College.
Inscribed on front: A long verse as shown in illustration.

height   202mm.   Price   £1,000

This model is multi-coloured.

No. 481. William of Wykeham

Inscribed on front: William of Wykeham founder of Winchester College 1393.

height   202mm.   Price   £1,000

This model is multi-coloured.

(Illustration by courtesy of City Museum and Art Gallery, Stoke-on-Trent).

No. 482. Witch's Cauldron

Inscribed as shown on illustration.

diameter of rim 57mm. Price £7.50

Identical in design to No. 226 Peterborough Tripod.

No. 483. Yorick's Skull

Inscribed on front as illustrated.

(a) pale yellow height 36mm. Price £30
(b) yellow or white height 70mm. Price £95
(c) white and in the height 100mm. Price £125
    form of a night-
    light

No. 484. Beccles Ringer's Jug

Inscription on base: The Ringers Jug in Beccles Parish Church. The original was made by Samuel Stringfellow, Potter. Inscribed on front as shown in illustration.

height 87mm. Price £300

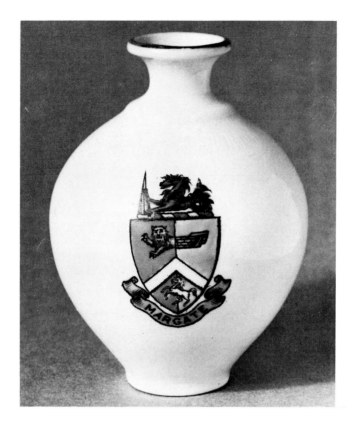

No. 485. Cliftonville Vase

Inscribed: Model of Roman vase found during excavations in Avenue Gardens, Cliftonville 1924.

height 106mm. Price £80

No. 486. Stratford Sanctuary Knocker

Inscribed: Model of the Stratford-on-Avon Sanctuary Knocker. Copyright.

height 71mm. Price £100

Marks

Many marks were used by the W.H. Goss firm but as far as this book is concerned the one illustrated is always shown although on the very late models the word 'ENGLAND' is printed below 'W.H. GOSS'. On the earliest models an impression of the firm's name is often found, but it is always accompanied by the mark illustrated.

Appendix

Although it was the intention not to show models marked "GOSS ENGLAND" in this Price Guide, the following have been included:

BANBURY CROSS. See No. 360
EDITH CAVELL MONUMENT. See No. 376
HINDHEAD SAILOR'S STONE. See No. 383
JOHN KNOX'S HOUSE. See No. 441

Alphabetical List of Contents

*These three models have only recently come to light and are therefore not included in the first section of the book.

The following two models were at one time reported to be 'in preparation', but it is now believed that they were not commercially produced or put on sale to the public.

Coloured   (a)   Atlantic View Hotel, Land's End
                (b)   Plas Newydd, Llangollen

Later Issues

After transfer of the firm, from the Goss family, new models were made for some time. All these carried the word 'ENGLAND' below the usual mark, an interesting point being that these were the only Goss pieces to do so.

Occasionally these later pieces have the word 'ENGLAND' missing. They can be identified by the fact that the base is indented in almost every case, and this forms a rim, the indentation being glazed and the rim unglazed.

Although it was not intended that this book should contain these late pieces they have been listed in the appendix, to make it as complete as possible.

Earlier pieces intended for export were marked 'EXPORTE ANGLETERRE', and usually bring a slightly higher price.